30-MINUTE

MEDITERRANEAN DIET

100 Quick, Crispy Healthy Recipes

AIR FRYER

2000 DAYS

FULL-COLOR EDITION

35-DAY MEAL PLAN

The 30-Minute Mediterranean Diet Air Fryer Cookbook for Beginners

100 Quick, Crispy, and Healthy Recipes to Boost Your Healthy Lifestyle. 35-Day Meal Plan Included

CONTENT

CHICKEN AND TURKEY 64

FISH AND SEAFOOD 85

VEGETABLES 96

APPETIZER 107

DESSERTS 118

CONCLUSION 129

Introduction

Starting a healthy lifestyle begins with the food you eat. To help you on your journey, I'm excited to share some of my favorite Mediterranean diet recipes, all made using an air fryer. I'll also guide you on how to use the Mediterranean food pyramid to build meals that nourish your body while satisfying your cravings guilt-free.

If you own an air fryer, you might have bought it to enjoy low-fat versions of your favorite fried foods. But the air fryer isn't just a replacement for deep frying—it's a versatile kitchen tool that lets you cook a wide range of foods more easily, in less time, and with less mess than traditional cooking methods.

In this book, I'll help you understand the basics of Mediterranean eating and show you how to use your air fryer to its full potential. You'll learn how to keep the fresh flavors and health benefits of Mediterranean cooking while using methods like roasting, grilling, and baking—all with your air fryer. Most importantly, you'll discover how cooking Mediterranean-style with an air fryer can make it easy and delicious to reach your health goals.

What is the Mediterranean Diet?

The Mediterranean diet is based on the traditional eating habits of people in southern Europe, especially Greece and Italy. While it became popular in the 1990s, it's been a way of life in those regions for centuries.

This diet focuses on eating lots of plant-based foods like whole grains, legumes, vegetables, fruits, and nuts, along with healthy fats such as olive oil. Fish and seafood are encouraged, while dairy, poultry, and red meat are eaten in moderation for optimal health.

The Mediterranean diet avoids processed foods, sugars, and white flour, making it easy and enjoyable to follow. Because it's not overly restrictive and offers proven health benefits, many people adopt this diet without feeling deprived. Plus, it allows for the occasional treat like dark chocolate, honey, or a glass of wine, which adds to its appeal.

High in fiber from whole grains and healthy fats, the Mediterranean diet helps you feel full longer and can aid in weight loss. When combined with protein-rich foods like legumes, nuts, seeds, and nutrient-dense vegetables, this diet offers a balanced and healthy way to eat and live.

Mediterranean Diet

The Mediterranean diet is one of the three diets recommended by the U.S. Dietary Guidelines and is recognized by both the American Heart Association and the American Diabetes Association as a good choice for those with heart disease or diabetes.

The Mediterranean Food Pyramid

Anyone can enjoy the Mediterranean diet. It combines an active and social lifestyle with fresh, vibrant, and flavorful meals based on whole foods and natural ingredients. The air fryer fits perfectly with this lifestyle. It preserves the flavor and nutrients of your food while reducing cooking and cleanup time, so you can spend more time enjoying meals with loved ones.

The foundation of the Mediterranean Pyramid is made up of whole grains, legumes, vegetables, fruits, and healthy fats like olive oil. Eating these foods together provides a healthy balance of protein, carbs, fats, fiber, vitamins, and minerals.

Whole grains and legumes are the most common foods in the Mediterranean Pyramid, and for good reason. They provide long-lasting energy, help prevent overeating, reduce the risk of heart disease, and help regulate blood sugar levels. Whether it's a snack like Sweet Potato and Chickpea Patties or a meal like Beef and Feta Stuffed Zucchini, there are many delicious air fryer recipes that highlight these staples of the Mediterranean diet.

As you plan your meals, you'll find yourself adding colorful and tasty vegetables to your plate. Classic Mediterranean veggies like artichokes, squash, eggplant, tomatoes, leafy greens, olives, and peppers—along with plenty of garlic, onions, and herbs—are great for air frying. You can roast, bake, or steam them to get the most nutrition without getting stuck in a cooking rut.

In addition to vegetables, fruits are often added to Mediterranean meals. Whether as part of breakfast, a snack, or a flavor accent, fruits play a key role. Some favorite air fryer recipes include bursts of fruit flavor—like the sweetness of Bananas and Stuffed Figs or the tartness in Apple Chips. Sometimes, fruit takes center stage, like in Fig and Pistachio Frangipane Tart or Almond and Orange Biscotti.

The Health Benefits of the Mediterranean Diet

I t's important to highlight the many health benefits of the Mediterranean diet. This way of eating can help with sustainable weight loss and significantly reduce the risks of common health issues.

With a focus on healthier fats like olive oil and plant-based foods, the Mediterranean diet has been shown to lower the risk of heart disease and stroke. Olive oil is a monounsaturated fat, which the American Heart Association says can reduce bad cholesterol and lower the risk of heart disease. The high fiber content in this diet also helps lower the risk of diabetes. For those already dealing with heart disease or diabetes, the Mediterranean diet can help manage symptoms.

This diet is also great for improving digestion and overall gut health. Healthy fats can soothe an irritated digestive tract, and the fiber from whole grains, legumes, and vegetables, along with a reduction in dairy, meat, and processed foods, can boost healthy gut bacteria. This makes it easier for your body to process food and absorb nutrients.

Studies have shown that the Mediterranean diet can increase longevity, reduce the risk of Alzheimer's and dementia, reduce inflammation, and even help maintain muscle strength as you age. No matter your reason for adopting the Mediterranean diet, it's a delicious and easy way to eat healthily—even if you're busy.

Getting Started with the Air Fryer

If you're new to the air fryer, don't worry! It's an easy appliance to use, and I'm here to help you get the most out of it.

The air fryer is perfect for making the Mediterranean diet even easier to follow. You can quickly prepare delicious, perfectly cooked meals for your family, and cleanup is a breeze. Adding a crispy texture to foods like Mozzarella Sticks, Beef Kofta Kebabs, Lamb Gyros, or Zucchini and Parmesan Pancakes is simple with an air fryer. You don't need to rely on lots of oil and saturated fats to get that satisfying crunch.

The air fryer encourages variety by letting you cook in different ways, so your meals are always interesting and tasty. After buying an air fryer, consider getting baking pans, muffin tins, and casserole dishes that fit inside the basket.

The best part of making Mediterranean meals in your air fryer is that it frees up your time. Instead of spending hours in the kitchen, you can go for a walk, relax with a glass of wine, or spend more time with your family.

Beyond Frying: Baking, Grilling, and Roasting

The air fryer is a versatile appliance that can do more than just fry. It's great for baking muffins, grilling fish, and roasting vegetables. Some of my favorite ways to use the air fryer include making frittatas, grilling kebabs, making crispy flatbread pizza crust, and even air-popped snacks.

You can easily whip up quick, nutritious breakfasts like Mediterranean Breakfast Burritos or Greek Spinach and Feta Egg Bites in less than 15 minutes. The air fryer adds great flavor and saves time, making it easier to stick to a healthy eating plan.

With grill and skewer attachments, you can make dishes like Greek Pork Souvlaki without firing up a full-sized grill. This saves energy and keeps you on track with cooking healthy meals, even when you're short on time.

Cooking Tips for the Air Fryer

Whether you're new to air frying or looking for helpful tips, these step-by-step instructions will help you get great results every time.

1. **Read the Manual:** Each air fryer brand has unique features, so it's important to understand how to operate yours safely.

2. **Preheat the Air Fryer:** This ensures faster and more even cooking.

3. **Prep Ingredients Evenly:** Cut your ingredients into similar sizes for uniform cooking.

4. **Avoid Overcrowding:** Place food in a single layer, and cook in batches if needed for the best results.

5. **Monitor Cooking Times:** Follow recipe guidelines for temperature and time. Use a meat thermometer to ensure meats are cooked properly.

What Not to Cook in the Air Fryer:

- Avoid adding oils for deep frying.

- Soups, stews, and broths are not suitable for air frying.

- Wet batters may not set properly; use bread crumbs instead.

- Pasta and rice should be boiled on the stove.

Air Fryer Tips for Mediterranean Foods

The air fryer is perfect for making many Mediterranean dishes healthier. Here are some tips:

Always preheat your air fryer before adding food to the basket for even cooking.

Coat vegetables and meats with olive oil before cooking to add flavor and a crispy texture.

Don't overcrowd the basket. Cook in batches if needed to get the best results.

Spray the food with cooking oil halfway through longer cooking times to keep it crispy.

Use a meat thermometer to ensure meats are cooked to the right temperature.

Turn food halfway through the cooking time if you want even grill marks when using a grill pan attachment.

Stocking Your Mediterranean, Air-Frying Kitchen

Being prepared is key to sticking with a healthy diet. Here's a list of Mediterranean diet staples to keep on hand in your pantry, fridge, and freezer:

Olive oil: Stock up on regular and spray varieties.

Whole grains and flours: Keep farro, quinoa, oats, brown rice, and wild rice, plus whole wheat flour, bread, and bread crumbs.

Legumes and pulses: Have chickpeas, lentils, and white beans on hand.

Herbs and spices: Stock dried and fresh herbs like basil, oregano, thyme, and garlic powder.

Fresh vegetables: Load up on bell peppers, broccoli, carrots, mushrooms, peas, potatoes, sweet potatoes, tomatoes, and zucchini.

Onions: Keep a variety like red onions, scallions, and yellow onions.

Garlic: Essential in all Mediterranean dishes.

Lemons: Great for adding brightness to recipes.

Fruits: Keep fresh or dried apples, apricots, and berries.

Shrimp: Great for quick meals, whether fresh or frozen.

Chicken breasts: A versatile protein that works well in the air fryer.

Eggs: Useful for breakfast, snacks, and many recipes.

Feta cheese: Perfect for salads, pita sandwiches, and more.

Greek yogurt: Ideal for drizzling on veggies or making sauces.

Honey: A natural sweetener that can be used in moderation.

Nuts and seeds: Keep walnuts, cashews, almonds, and sunflower seeds for snacking or adding crunch to dishes.

Choosing Healthy Oils

Olive oil is the go-to oil in Mediterranean cooking. Choose high-quality extra-virgin olive oil for the best flavor. Look for a bottle with a harvest date no more than a year before your purchase. A dark bottle will help protect the oil from light.

Use olive oil to drizzle over or coat ingredients before air frying, and don't forget olive-oil-based nonstick spray for preventing food from sticking.

Other Kitchen Essentials

While your air fryer is a key tool, there are a few other items you should have in your kitchen:

- A chef's knife and cutting board.

- Mixing bowls, measuring spoons, measuring cups, and a liquid measuring cup.

- Baking pans, muffin tins, and casserole dishes that fit in your air fryer.

- A whisk, tongs, a spatula, and wooden spoons for cooking and serving.

- Airtight glass storage containers for leftovers, and Mason jars for storage.

- A garlic press for quick mincing.

- A food processor for chopping and mixing ingredients.

Recipes for Success

The recipes in this book are designed to be easy and delicious, fitting perfectly within the Mediterranean diet guidelines. You'll find options for vegetarian, gluten-free, and even vegan meals. There are also many roasted, baked, and grilled recipes that offer variety and a taste of the Mediterranean.

With the air fryer, you'll enjoy fast and flavorful meals with less hassle. These recipes will help you stay on track with your health goals while satisfying your cravings. My goal is to give you not only delicious recipes but also a new way to enjoy cooking!

35 DAYS MEAL PLAN

Meal Plan

Sun		
Mon		
Tue		
Wed		
Thu		
Fri		
Sat		

35 Days Meal Plan

DAY	BREAKFAST	LUNCH	DINNER
monday	Mediterranean Breakfast Burritos	Greek-Style Pork Chops	Lemon and Herb Sardines
tuesday	Mediterranean Veggie Frittata	Mediterranean Herb Chicken	Quinoa and Black Bean Stuffed Peppers
wednesday	Shakshuka with Eggs	Beef Kofta Kebabs	Shrimp and Feta Orzo
thursday	Halloumi and Tomato Toasts	Moroccan Chicken Drumsticks	Stuffed Squid
friday	Baked Eggs with Herbs	Greek Lamb Pie	Vegan Spanakopita
saturday	Mediterranean Omelet Cups	Chicken Caprese	Lemon Herb Cod
sunday	Banana & Nut Oatmeal Cups	Lamb Gyros	Cauliflower Steaks with Tahini Drizzle

35 Days Meal Plan

DAY	BREAKFAST	LUNCH	DINNER
monday	Honey and Nut Granola Clusters	Spiced Turkey Patties with Pepper Sauce	Tilapia with Olive Tapenade
tuesday	Greek Spinach and Feta Egg Bites	Beef and Feta Stuffed Zucchini	Vegan Moussaka
wednesday	Greek-Style Air-Fried Pancakes	Chicken and Olive Tagine	Asparagus with Almond Crumbs
thursday	Falafel Breakfast Wraps	Lamb Stuffed Eggplant	Tuna Steaks with Capers
friday	Zucchini and Feta Breakfast Hash	Mediterranean Vegetables with Lamb	Broccoli with Garlic and Parmesan
saturday	Sundried Tomato and Olive Quiche	Greek Turkey Meatballs	Herb Fish Cakes
sunday	Spinach and Artichoke Frittata	Garlic and Herb Turkey Tenderloin	Stuffed Artichokes with Lemon and Herbs

35 Days Meal Plan

DAY	BREAKFAST	LUNCH	DINNER
monday	Spinach and Lemon Hummus Egg Wraps	Paprika and Lime Chicken Drumsticks	Halibut with Garlic Lemon Aioli
tuesday	Turkish Eggs with Greek Yogurt	Mediterranean Style Pork Ribs	Vegan Mushroom Gyros
wednesday	Mediterranean Breakfast Potatoes	Beef Lasagna	Anchovy and Tomato Crostini
thursday	Smashed Egg Toasts with Herby Lemon Yogurt	Lemon Garlic Rosemary Turkey Breasts	Sweet Potato and Chickpea Patties
friday	Chickpeas and Scrambled Eggs with Garlicky Greens and Yogurt	Shawarma-Style Chicken	Fish Tacos with Yogurt Sauce
saturday	Zucchini and Parmesan Pancakes	Mediterranean Beef Patties	Cheesy Topped Mediterranean Pork Loin Chops
sunday	Mediterranean Breakfast Burritos	Spiced Lamb Ribs	Stuffed Squid

35 Days Meal Plan

DAY	BREAKFAST	LUNCH	DINNER
monday	Mediterranean Veggie Frittata	Turkey Croquettes with Dip	Vegan Spanakopita
tuesday	Shakshuka with Eggs	Chicken and Artichoke Hearts	Lemon and Herb Sardines
wednesday	Halloumi and Tomato Toasts	Ground Turkey with Vegetables	Cauliflower Steaks with Tahini Drizzle
thursday	Baked Eggs with Herbs	Greek Pork Souvlaki	Herb Fish Cakes
friday	Mediterranean Omelet Cups	Lamb and Pine Nut Mini Pies	Tilapia with Olive Tapenade
saturday	Banana & Nut Oatmeal Cups	Steak Bites with Yogurt Sauce	Stuffed Artichokes with Lemon and Herbs
sunday	Honey and Nut Granola Clusters	Chicken Parmesan	Shrimp and Feta Orzo

 # 35 Days Meal Plan

DAY	BREAKFAST	LUNCH	DINNER
monday	Greek Spinach and Feta Egg Bites	Beef Chops Stuffed with Spinach and Feta	Quinoa and Black Bean Stuffed Peppers
tuesday	Greek-Style Air-Fried Pancakes	Mediterranean Turkey Salad	Mediterranean Chicken Cordon Bleu
wednesday	Falafel Breakfast Wraps	Turkey and Spinach Pinwheels	Lamb Chops with Rosemary
thursday	Zucchini and Feta Breakfast Hash	Garlic and Herb Turkey Tenderloin	Beef Meatballs
friday	Sundried Tomato and Olive Quiche	Mediterranean Pork Tenderloin Crostini	Halibut with Garlic Lemon Aioli
saturday	Spinach and Artichoke Frittata	Turkey and Vegetable Skewers with Tomato Sauce	Beef and Feta Stuffed Zucchini
sunday	Spinach and Lemon Hummus Egg Wraps	Mediterranean Chicken Cordon Bleu	Lamb Stuffed Eggplant

BREAKFAST

Mediterranean Breakfast Burritos

Breakfast burritos are a delicious way to combine the flavors of the Mediterranean diet with a popular American breakfast option. The concept of wrapping food in flatbreads dates back to ancient civilizations, including those in the Mediterranean region. By using whole wheat tortillas and fresh ingredients like spinach, cherry tomatoes, and avocado, this recipe not only provides a nutritious start to your day but also pays homage to the Mediterranean tradition of wholesome, balanced meals. The air fryer adds a modern twist by making the cooking process faster and healthier.

Nutrition Cal 280; Protein 16 g; Fat 20 g; Carb; 7 g

Instructions

1. Preheat your air fryer to 350°F (175°C).
2. In a medium bowl, whisk the eggs until well blended. Add the cherry tomatoes, spinach, red bell pepper, red onion, dried oregano, salt, and pepper. Mix until all ingredients are combined.
3. Grease a small oven-safe dish or air fryer baking pan with olive oil.
4. Pour the egg mixture into the prepared dish.
5. Place the dish in the air fryer basket. Cook for 10-12 minutes, or until the eggs are set.
6. Warm the whole wheat tortillas in the air fryer for about 2 minutes.
7. Remove the egg mixture and tortillas from the air fryer.
8. Evenly divide the egg mixture between the two tortillas. Top each with feta cheese and avocado slices.
9. Roll up the tortillas to form burritos.
10. Place the burritos back in the air fryer basket and cook for an additional 2-3 minutes to crisp up the tortilla.
11. Serve warm.

 Prep time: 10 min

 Cook time: 20 min

 Servings: 2

Ingredients

- 4 large eggs
- 1/4 cup feta cheese, crumbled
- 1/2 cup cherry tomatoes, halved
- 1/2 cup spinach, chopped
- 1/4 cup red bell pepper, diced
- 1/4 cup red onion, finely chopped
- 1/2 tsp dried oregano
- 1/2 avocado, sliced
- 2 whole wheat tortillas
- Salt and pepper to taste

Mediterranean Veggie Frittata

Frittata, which means "fried" in Italian, has been a staple in Mediterranean cuisine for centuries. Traditionally, it's an open-faced omelet loaded with a variety of vegetables, meats, and cheeses. This versatile dish reflects the Mediterranean diet's emphasis on fresh, wholesome ingredients and its roots in resourceful, peasant cooking where nothing goes to waste. The air fryer modernizes this classic dish by reducing cooking time and minimizing the need for added oils, making it a perfect fit for today's health-conscious cooks.

Nutrition Cal 350; Protein 18 g; Fat 22 g; Carb; 24 g

Instructions

1. Preheat your air fryer to 350°F (175°C).
2. In a medium bowl, whisk the eggs until well blended. Add the feta cheese, cherry tomatoes, spinach, red bell pepper, red onion, dried oregano, salt, and pepper. Mix until all ingredients are combined.
3. Grease a small oven-safe dish or air fryer baking pan with olive oil.
4. Pour the egg mixture into the prepared dish.
5. Place the dish in the air fryer basket. Cook for 15-20 minutes, or until the frittata is set and the top is golden brown.
6. Remove the frittata from the air fryer and let it cool for a few minutes before slicing.
7. Serve warm.

 Prep time: 10 min

 Cook time: 20 min

 Servings: 2

Ingredients

- 4 large eggs
- 1/4 cup feta cheese, crumbled
- 1/2 cup cherry tomatoes, halved
- 1/2 cup spinach, chopped
- 1/4 cup red bell pepper, diced
- 1/4 cup red onion, finely chopped
- 1/2 tsp dried oregano
- Salt and pepper to taste
- 1 tbsp olive oil

Shakshuka with Eggs

Shakshuka is a traditional North African and Middle Eastern dish that has become a beloved breakfast staple in Mediterranean cuisine. The name "shakshuka" means "a mixture" in Arabic, reflecting its simple yet flavorful blend of ingredients. This dish, rich in vegetables and spices, highlights the Mediterranean diet's focus on fresh, wholesome ingredients. Traditionally cooked in a skillet, air-frying shakshuka offers a modern twist, making it a quick and healthy option for busy mornings while retaining its authentic, hearty flavors.

Nutrition Cal 300; Protein 14 g; Fat 20 g; Carb; 18 g

Instructions

1. Preheat your air fryer to 350°F (175°C).
2. In a medium-sized oven-safe dish or air fryer baking pan, heat the olive oil. Add the chopped onion and red bell pepper, and cook for 3-5 minutes until softened.
3. Add the minced garlic, ground cumin, smoked paprika, ground coriander, and red pepper flakes (if using). Cook for another 2 minutes until fragrant.
4. Add the diced tomatoes, salt, and pepper. Stir well to combine.
5. Cook the tomato mixture in the air fryer for 10 minutes until it thickens slightly.
6. Make four small wells in the tomato mixture and crack an egg into each well.
7. Return the dish to the air fryer and cook for another 8-10 minutes, or until the egg whites are set but the yolks are still runny.
8. Remove the dish from the air fryer and sprinkle with crumbled feta cheese and fresh parsley or cilantro.
9. Serve warm with crusty bread or pita.

 Prep time: 10 min

 Cook time: 20 min

 Servings: 2

Ingredients

- 1 tbsp olive oil
- 1 small onion, finely chopped
- 1 red bell pepper, diced
- 2 cloves garlic, minced
- 1 tsp ground cumin
- 1 tsp smoked paprika
- 1/2 tsp ground coriander
- 1/4 tsp red pepper flakes (optional)
- 1 can (14.5 oz) diced tomatoes
- Salt and pepper to taste
- 4 large eggs
- 1/4 cup crumbled feta cheese
- Fresh parsley or cilantro for garnish

Halloumi and Tomato Toasts

Halloumi cheese, originating from Cyprus, is known for its high melting point, making it ideal for grilling and frying. Its unique texture and salty flavor have made it a popular ingredient in Mediterranean cuisine. This recipe showcases the versatility of halloumi, combining it with juicy cherry tomatoes and hearty whole grain bread to create a delicious and balanced meal. The use of an air fryer not only makes this dish quick and easy to prepare but also enhances the flavors by giving the halloumi a perfect crispiness and the tomatoes a delightful roast.

Nutrition Cal 320; Protein 15 g; Fat 21 g; Carb; 22 g

Instructions

1. Preheat your air fryer to 375°F (190°C).
2. In a bowl, toss the cherry tomatoes with olive oil, minced garlic, dried oregano, salt, and pepper.
3. Arrange the halloumi slices and seasoned cherry tomatoes in the air fryer basket. Cook for 10 minutes, shaking the basket halfway through to ensure even cooking.
4. While the halloumi and tomatoes are cooking, toast the whole grain bread slices in a toaster or on a pan until golden brown.
5. Once the halloumi and tomatoes are done, assemble the toasts by placing slices of halloumi on each piece of toasted bread. Top with the roasted cherry tomatoes.
6. Garnish with fresh basil leaves and serve warm.

 Prep time: 10 min

 Cook time: 15 min

 Servings: 2

Ingredients

- 4 slices whole grain bread
- 8 oz halloumi cheese, sliced
- 1 cup cherry tomatoes, halved
- 1 tbsp olive oil
- 1 clove garlic, minced
- 1/2 tsp dried oregano
- Salt and pepper to taste
- Fresh basil leaves for garnish

Baked Eggs with Herbs

Baked eggs, also known as "shirred eggs," have been enjoyed since the 18th century in both French and English cuisines. The term "shirred" comes from the type of dish in which the eggs are traditionally baked. This recipe embodies the Mediterranean diet's emphasis on fresh herbs and simple, wholesome ingredients. By using an air fryer, this dish becomes even more convenient to prepare, offering a quick yet elegant breakfast or brunch option that is rich in flavor and nutrients.

Nutrition Cal 250; Protein 16 g; Fat 18 g; Carb; 4 g

Instructions

1. Preheat your air fryer to 350°F (175°C).
2. Grease two small oven-safe ramekins or baking dishes with olive oil.
3. Crack two eggs into each ramekin.
4. Pour half of the milk or cream into each ramekin, over the eggs.
5. Sprinkle the grated Parmesan cheese evenly over the eggs.
6. Add the chopped parsley, chives, dill, salt, and pepper on top.
7. Place the ramekins in the air fryer basket and cook for 12-15 minutes, or until the egg whites are set and the yolks are cooked to your desired level.
8. Carefully remove the ramekins from the air fryer and let them cool for a minute before serving.

 Prep time: 5 min

 Cook time: 15 min

 Servings: 2

Ingredients

- 4 large eggs
- 1/4 cup milk or cream
- 1/4 cup grated Parmesan cheese
- 1 tbsp fresh parsley, chopped
- 1 tbsp fresh chives, chopped
- 1 tbsp fresh dill, chopped
- Salt and pepper to taste
- 1 tbsp olive oil

Mediterranean Omelet Cups

Omelet cups are a modern twist on the classic omelet, perfect for busy mornings or meal prep. The Mediterranean diet, known for its heart-healthy benefits, emphasizes fresh vegetables and lean proteins. This recipe captures the essence of Mediterranean cuisine with ingredients like spinach, feta cheese, and cherry tomatoes, all packed into a convenient, portable breakfast option. Air frying these omelet cups not only speeds up the cooking process but also ensures a light and fluffy texture without the need for excessive oil.

Nutrition Cal 290; Protein 17 g; Fat 22 g; Carb; 6 g

Instructions

1. Preheat your air fryer to 350°F (175°C).
2. In a medium bowl, whisk together the eggs and milk until well blended.
3. Add the feta cheese, spinach, cherry tomatoes, red bell pepper, red onion, dried oregano, salt, and pepper to the egg mixture. Stir to combine.
4. Grease a muffin tin or silicone muffin cups with olive oil.
5. Pour the egg mixture evenly into the prepared muffin cups, filling each about 3/4 full.
6. Place the muffin tin or silicone cups in the air fryer basket.
7. Cook for 15-20 minutes, or until the omelet cups are set and lightly golden on top.
8. Remove the omelet cups from the air fryer and let them cool for a few minutes before serving.

 Prep time: 10 min

 Cook time: 20 min

 Servings: 2

Ingredients

- 4 large eggs
- 1/4 cup milk or cream
- 1/4 cup feta cheese, crumbled
- 1/2 cup spinach, chopped
- 1/4 cup cherry tomatoes, halved
- 1/4 cup red bell pepper, diced
- 1/4 cup red onion, finely chopped
- 1/2 tsp dried oregano
- Salt and pepper to taste
- 1 tbsp olive oil

Banana & Nut Oatmeal Cups

Oatmeal has been a staple breakfast food for centuries, valued for its nutritional benefits and versatility. Bananas, originally from Southeast Asia, are now a key ingredient in many healthy recipes around the world. This recipe combines the heart-healthy benefits of oats with the natural sweetness of bananas and the crunch of nuts, making it a delicious and nutritious start to your day. Air frying these oatmeal cups provides a quick and convenient way to enjoy a baked breakfast treat without the need for a traditional oven, perfect for busy mornings or on-the-go snacks.

Nutrition Cal 300; Protein 6 g; Fat 12 g; Carb; 45 g

Instructions

1. Preheat your air fryer to 350°F (175°C).
2. In a large bowl, combine the rolled oats, mashed banana, milk, chopped nuts, honey or maple syrup, vanilla extract, cinnamon, and salt. Mix well until all ingredients are evenly incorporated. If using, fold in the dark chocolate chips.
3. Grease a muffin tin or silicone muffin cups with a little oil or non-stick spray.
4. Divide the mixture evenly among the prepared muffin cups, filling each about 3/4 full.
5. Place the muffin tin or silicone cups in the air fryer basket.
6. Cook for 15-20 minutes, or until the oatmeal cups are set and golden brown on top.
7. Remove the oatmeal cups from the air fryer and let them cool for a few minutes before serving.

 Prep time: 10 min

 Cook time: 20 min

 Servings: 2

Ingredients

- 1 cup rolled oats
- 1/2 cup mashed ripe banana (about 1 large banana)
- 1/2 cup milk or almond milk
- 1/4 cup chopped nuts (walnuts, almonds, or pecans)
- 1/4 cup honey or maple syrup
- 1 tsp vanilla extract
- 1/2 tsp cinnamon
- 1/4 tsp salt
- 1/4 cup dark chocolate chips (optional)

Honey and Nut Granola Clusters

Granola, originally created in the late 19th century, was first known as "granula" and was a staple in health food movements. The combination of oats, nuts, and honey not only provides a deliciously sweet and crunchy snack but also packs a punch of nutrients essential for a balanced diet. The Mediterranean diet emphasizes nuts and natural sweeteners like honey, which are both prominent in this recipe. Air frying granola clusters offers a quick and efficient way to achieve a perfect crunch without the need for long baking times, making it a convenient option for a healthy breakfast or snack.

Nutrition Cal 350; Protein 6 g; Fat 22 g; Carb; 32 g

Instructions

1. Preheat your air fryer to 325°F (160°C).
2. In a large bowl, combine the rolled oats, mixed nuts, honey, melted coconut oil, vanilla extract, cinnamon, and salt. Mix until all ingredients are well coated.
3. If using, fold in the dried fruit.
4. Line the air fryer basket with parchment paper or a silicone mat.
5. Drop spoonfuls of the mixture onto the prepared basket, forming small clusters. Press them together slightly to help them hold their shape.
6. Cook in the air fryer for 10-15 minutes, or until the clusters are golden brown and crisp. Shake the basket halfway through cooking to ensure even baking.
7. Allow the granola clusters to cool completely before removing from the air fryer. They will firm up as they cool.
8. Store in an airtight container for up to a week.

 Prep time: 10 min

 Cook time: 15 min

 Servings: 2

Ingredients

- 1 cup rolled oats
- 1/2 cup mixed nuts (almonds, walnuts, pecans), roughly chopped
- 1/4 cup honey
- 2 tbsp coconut oil, melted
- 1/2 tsp vanilla extract
- 1/2 tsp cinnamon
- 1/4 tsp salt
- 1/4 cup dried fruit (raisins, cranberries, or apricots), optional

Greek Spinach and Feta Egg Bites

Spinach and feta are classic ingredients in Greek cuisine, often found in dishes like spanakopita, a savory pastry filled with spinach and cheese. This combination not only delivers a burst of flavor but also provides a nutritious boost, as spinach is rich in iron and vitamins, while feta adds calcium and protein. These air-fried egg bites are a modern take on these traditional flavors, offering a convenient and healthy option for breakfast or a quick snack. The air fryer ensures they are cooked evenly and quickly, making them perfect for busy mornings.

Nutrition   Cal 250; Protein 15 g; Fat 18 g; Carb; 6 g

Instructions

1. Preheat your air fryer to 350°F (175°C).
2. In a medium bowl, whisk together the eggs and milk until well blended.
3. Add the chopped spinach, feta cheese, red bell pepper, red onion, minced garlic, dried oregano, salt, and pepper to the egg mixture. Stir to combine.
4. Grease silicone muffin cups or a muffin tin with olive oil.
5. Pour the egg mixture evenly into the prepared muffin cups, filling each about 3/4 full.
6. Place the muffin cups in the air fryer basket.
7. Cook for 12-15 minutes, or until the egg bites are set and lightly golden on top.
8. Remove the egg bites from the air fryer and let them cool for a few minutes before serving.

 Prep time: 10 min

 Cook time: 15 min

 Servings: 2

Ingredients

- 4 large eggs
- 1/4 cup milk or cream
- 1/2 cup fresh spinach, chopped
- 1/4 cup feta cheese, crumbled
- 1/4 cup red bell pepper, finely diced
- 1/4 cup red onion, finely chopped
- 1 clove garlic, minced
- 1/2 tsp dried oregano
- Salt and pepper to taste
- 1 tbsp olive oil

Greek-Style Air-Fried Pancakes

Greek cuisine often incorporates yogurt and honey, both of which are staples in the Mediterranean diet. Greek yogurt, known for its thick and creamy texture, adds a rich flavor and a boost of protein to these pancakes, while honey provides natural sweetness. These pancakes are a nutritious twist on traditional recipes, packed with the goodness of whole grains, nuts, and fresh fruit. Cooking them in an air fryer not only speeds up the process but also ensures a fluffy texture with minimal added fat, making them a perfect healthy breakfast option.

Nutrition Cal 320; Protein 10 g; Fat 14 g; Carb; 40 g

Instructions

1. Preheat your air fryer to 350°F (175°C).
2. In a large bowl, whisk together the whole wheat flour, baking powder, and salt.
3. In another bowl, mix the honey or maple syrup, Greek yogurt, milk, egg, and vanilla extract until well combined.
4. Pour the wet ingredients into the dry ingredients and stir until just combined. Do not overmix.
5. Gently fold in the chopped walnuts and fresh blueberries.
6. Grease silicone muffin cups or a small oven-safe dish with olive oil spray.
7. Pour the batter evenly into the prepared cups or dish, filling each about 3/4 full.
8. Place the cups or dish in the air fryer basket.
9. Cook for 12-15 minutes, or until the pancakes are set and lightly golden on top. A toothpick inserted into the center should come out clean.
10. Remove from the air fryer and let cool for a few minutes before serving.

 Prep time: 10 min

 Cook time: 15 min

 Servings: 2

Ingredients

- 1 cup whole wheat flour
- 1 tbsp baking powder
- 1/4 tsp salt
- 1 tbsp honey or maple syrup
- 1 cup Greek yogurt
- 1/4 cup milk
- 1 large egg
- 1/2 tsp vanilla extract
- 1/2 cup chopped walnuts
- 1/2 cup fresh blueberries
- Olive oil spray for greasing

Falafel Breakfast Wraps

Greek cuisine often incorporates yogurt and honey, both of which are staples in the Mediterranean diet. Greek yogurt, known for its thick and creamy texture, adds a rich flavor and a boost of protein to these pancakes, while honey provides natural sweetness. These pancakes are a nutritious twist on traditional recipes, packed with the goodness of whole grains, nuts, and fresh fruit. Cooking them in an air fryer not only speeds up the process but also ensures a fluffy texture with minimal added fat, making them a perfect healthy breakfast option.

Nutrition Cal 400; Protein 14 g; Fat 20 g; Carb; 40 g

Instructions

1. Preheat your air fryer to 375°F (190°C).
2. In a food processor, combine the chickpeas, red onion, garlic, parsley, cumin, coriander, baking powder, flour, salt, and pepper. Pulse until the mixture is well combined but still slightly chunky.
3. Form the mixture into small patties or balls, about 1 inch in diameter.
4. Brush or spray the falafel with olive oil.
5. Place the falafel in the air fryer basket in a single layer. Cook for 12-15 minutes, turning halfway through, until they are golden brown and crispy.

Assemble the Wraps:

1. Warm the whole wheat tortillas in the air fryer for about 1-2 minutes until they are pliable.
2. Spread a generous amount of hummus on each tortilla.
3. Place a few falafel patties in the center of each tortilla.
4. Top with cherry tomatoes, cucumber slices, red onion, feta cheese, and spinach leaves.
5. Drizzle with tahini sauce if desired.
6. Roll up the tortillas tightly to form wraps.
7. Cut the wraps in half and serve warm.

 Prep time: 15 min

 Cook time: 15 min

 Servings: 2

Ingredients

For the Falafel:
- 1 cup canned chickpeas, drained and rinsed
- 1/4 cup red onion, finely chopped
- 2 cloves garlic, minced
- 1/4 cup fresh parsley, chopped
- 1 tsp ground cumin
- 1 tsp ground coriander
- 1/2 tsp baking powder
- 1 tbsp flour (whole wheat or chickpea)
- Salt and pepper to taste
- 1 tbsp olive oil

For the Wrap:
- 2 large whole wheat tortillas
- 1/2 cup hummus
- 1/2 cup cherry tomatoes, halved
- 1/2 cup cucumber, sliced
- 1/4 cup red onion, thinly sliced
- 1/4 cup feta cheese, crumbled
- 1/4 cup fresh spinach leaves
- 1 tbsp tahini sauce (optional)

Zucchini and Feta Breakfast Hash

Zucchini, also known as courgette, is a versatile summer squash that is a staple in Mediterranean cuisine. It is low in calories but rich in vitamins and antioxidants. This breakfast hash combines the mild flavor of zucchini with the tanginess of feta cheese, offering a delicious and nutritious start to the day. Air frying the vegetables brings out their natural sweetness and ensures a quick, even cooking process. This dish highlights the Mediterranean diet's focus on fresh, wholesome ingredients, making it both healthy and satisfying.

Nutrition   Cal 280; Protein 14 g; Fat 20 g; Carb; 12 g

Instructions

1. Preheat your air fryer to 375°F (190°C).
2. In a large bowl, combine the diced zucchini, red bell pepper, red onion, and minced garlic.
3. Drizzle with olive oil and sprinkle with dried oregano, dried thyme, salt, and pepper. Toss to coat evenly.
4. Place the vegetable mixture in the air fryer basket in an even layer.
5. Cook for 10 minutes, shaking the basket halfway through cooking to ensure even browning.
6. After the vegetables have cooked for 10 minutes, create two small wells in the mixture and crack an egg into each well.
7. Continue to cook for another 5 minutes, or until the eggs are set to your desired doneness.
8. Carefully remove the basket from the air fryer. Sprinkle the crumbled feta cheese over the top of the hash.
9. Garnish with fresh parsley before serving.

 Prep time: 10 min

 Cook time: 15 min

 Servings: 2

Ingredients

- 2 medium zucchinis, diced
- 1 small red bell pepper, diced
- 1 small red onion, finely chopped
- 2 cloves garlic, minced
- 1 tbsp olive oil
- 1/2 tsp dried oregano
- 1/2 tsp dried thyme
- Salt and pepper to taste
- 1/2 cup feta cheese, crumbled
- 2 large eggs
- Fresh parsley for garnish

Sundried Tomato and Olive Quiche

Quiche, a savory pie with a rich custard filling, originated in France but has become popular worldwide. This Mediterranean-inspired version incorporates classic flavors like sundried tomatoes, olives, and feta cheese, bringing a unique twist to the traditional dish. Sundried tomatoes add a concentrated burst of flavor and nutrients, while olives contribute healthy fats and a distinctive taste. Cooking the quiche in an air fryer not only speeds up the process but also creates a perfectly cooked, creamy filling with a golden crust, making it an ideal dish for a quick and satisfying breakfast or brunch.

Nutrition Cal 350; Protein 16 g; Fat 25 g; Carb; 15 g

Instructions

1. Preheat your air fryer to 350°F (175°C).
2. In a medium bowl, whisk together the eggs and milk (or cream) until well blended.
3. Add the feta cheese, sundried tomatoes, black olives, spinach, red onion, minced garlic, dried oregano, salt, and pepper. Mix until all ingredients are evenly distributed.
4. If using a pre-made pie crust, fit it into a small, oven-safe dish that fits into your air fryer basket.
5. Pour the egg mixture into the pie crust. If making a crustless quiche, simply pour the mixture into a greased oven-safe dish.
6. Place the dish in the air fryer basket.
7. Cook for 15-20 minutes, or until the quiche is set and the top is lightly golden. A toothpick inserted into the center should come out clean.
8. Remove the quiche from the air fryer and let it cool for a few minutes before slicing.
9. Serve warm.

 Prep time: 15 min

 Cook time: 20 min

 Servings: 2

Ingredients

- 4 large eggs
- 1/2 cup milk or cream
- 1/2 cup feta cheese, crumbled
- 1/4 cup sundried tomatoes, chopped
- 1/4 cup black olives, sliced
- 1/4 cup spinach, chopped
- 1/4 cup red onion, finely chopped
- 1 clove garlic, minced
- 1/2 tsp dried oregano
- Salt and pepper to taste
- 1 tbsp olive oil
- 1 pre-made pie crust (or use a crustless option for a lighter version)

Spinach and Artichoke Frittata

Frittatas are an Italian dish similar to an omelet but are typically cooked slowly over low heat and finished in the oven. This method creates a fluffy and custard-like texture. This Mediterranean-inspired frittata combines the earthy flavors of spinach and artichokes with the tangy taste of feta cheese. Spinach and artichokes are both nutrient-dense vegetables that provide a range of vitamins and minerals. The air fryer speeds up the cooking process, making it easier to enjoy a healthy and delicious breakfast or brunch without the need for extensive cooking techniques.

Nutrition   Cal 270; Protein 16 g; Fat 20 g; Carb; 7 g

Instructions

1. Preheat your air fryer to 350°F (175°C).
2. In a medium bowl, whisk together the eggs and milk (or cream) until well blended.
3. Add the chopped artichoke hearts, spinach, feta cheese, red onion, minced garlic, dried oregano, salt, and pepper. Mix until all ingredients are evenly distributed.
4. Grease a small, oven-safe dish or air fryer baking pan with olive oil.
5. Pour the egg mixture into the prepared dish.
6. Place the dish in the air fryer basket.
7. Cook for 12-15 minutes, or until the frittata is set and the top is lightly golden. A toothpick inserted into the center should come out clean.
8. Remove the frittata from the air fryer and let it cool for a few minutes before slicing.
9. Serve warm.

 Prep time: 10 min

 Cook time: 15 min

 Servings: 2

Ingredients

- 4 large eggs
- 1/4 cup milk or cream
- 1/2 cup artichoke hearts, drained and chopped
- 1/2 cup fresh spinach, chopped
- 1/4 cup feta cheese, crumbled
- 1/4 cup red onion, finely chopped
- 1 clove garlic, minced
- 1/2 tsp dried oregano
- Salt and pepper to taste
- 1 tbsp olive oil

Spinach and Lemon Hummus Egg Wraps

Hummus, a creamy spread made from chickpeas, tahini, lemon juice, and garlic, has been a staple in Middle Eastern and Mediterranean diets for centuries. It's known for its high protein and fiber content, making it a nutritious addition to any meal. Combining hummus with eggs and fresh vegetables in this wrap creates a balanced and flavorful breakfast or lunch option. The air fryer not only cooks the eggs quickly but also ensures they are perfectly set, making assembly of these delicious wraps a breeze.

Nutrition   Cal 320; Protein 17 g; Fat 18 g; Carb; 24 g

Instructions

1. Preheat your air fryer to 350°F (175°C).
2. In a medium bowl, whisk together the eggs and milk (or cream) until well blended.
3. Add the chopped spinach, red bell pepper, red onion, minced garlic, dried oregano, salt, and pepper. Mix until all ingredients are evenly distributed.
4. Grease a small oven-safe dish or air fryer baking pan with olive oil spray.
5. Pour the egg mixture into the prepared dish.
6. Place the dish in the air fryer basket.
7. Cook for 8-10 minutes, or until the eggs are set and lightly golden.
8. Warm the whole wheat tortillas in the air fryer for about 1-2 minutes until they are pliable.
9. Spread a generous amount of lemon hummus on each tortilla.
10. Divide the cooked egg mixture between the two tortillas, placing it in the center of each.
11. Roll up the tortillas tightly to form wraps.
12. Cut the wraps in half and serve warm.

 Prep time: 10 min

 Cook time: 10 min

 Servings: 2

Ingredients

- 4 large eggs
- 1/4 cup milk or cream
- 1/2 cup fresh spinach, chopped
- 1/4 cup lemon hummus
- 1/4 cup red bell pepper, diced
- 1/4 cup red onion, finely chopped
- 1 clove garlic, minced
- 1/2 tsp dried oregano
- Salt and pepper to taste
- 2 large whole wheat tortillas
- Olive oil spray

Turkish Eggs with Greek Yogurt

Turkish eggs, or "Çılbır," is a traditional Turkish dish that dates back to the Ottoman Empire. It's a savory combination of poached eggs served over a bed of garlicky yogurt, drizzled with spiced butter or olive oil. This dish is a perfect example of the Mediterranean diet, emphasizing fresh herbs, yogurt, and healthy fats. By using an air fryer to cook the eggs, this modern twist ensures a quick and easy preparation while maintaining the authentic flavors and textures of this beloved classic.

Nutrition Cal 350; Protein 17 g; Fat 25 g; Carb; 18 g

Instructions

1. In a medium bowl, combine the Greek yogurt, minced garlic, chopped dill, chopped parsley, salt, and pepper. Mix well and set aside.
2. Preheat your air fryer to 350°F (175°C).
3. Grease small, oven-safe dishes or ramekins with olive oil.
4. Crack two eggs into each dish.
5. Place the dishes in the air fryer basket and cook for 8-10 minutes, or until the egg whites are set and the yolks are cooked to your desired level of doneness.
6. In a small saucepan, heat the olive oil over medium heat.
7. Add the paprika and red pepper flakes, and stir for about 1 minute until fragrant. Remove from heat.
8. Spread the Greek yogurt mixture evenly on two serving plates.
9. Carefully place the cooked eggs on top of the yogurt.
10. Drizzle the spiced olive oil over the eggs and yogurt.
11. Serve with toasted whole grain bread on the side.

 Prep time: 10 min

 Cook time: 10 min

 Servings: 2

Ingredients

- 4 large eggs
- 1 cup Greek yogurt
- 2 cloves garlic, minced
- 1 tbsp fresh dill, chopped
- 1 tbsp fresh parsley, chopped
- 1/4 cup olive oil
- 1 tsp paprika
- 1/2 tsp red pepper flakes
- Salt and pepper to taste
- 2 slices whole grain bread, toasted

Mediterranean Breakfast Potatoes

Potatoes have been a staple in Mediterranean cuisine since they were introduced to Europe in the 16th century. This breakfast dish combines the hearty comfort of potatoes with the vibrant flavors of the Mediterranean, including herbs and spices like oregano, smoked paprika, and cumin. The addition of feta cheese adds a tangy, creamy element that pairs perfectly with the crispy potatoes. Cooking the potatoes in an air fryer ensures they are crispy on the outside and tender on the inside, making for a delicious and healthy breakfast option.

Nutrition   Cal 300; Protein 6 g; Fat 14 g; Carb; 36 g

Instructions

1. Preheat your air fryer to 375°F (190°C).
2. In a large bowl, combine the diced potatoes, red bell pepper, red onion, and minced garlic.
3. Drizzle with olive oil and sprinkle with dried oregano, smoked paprika, ground cumin, salt, and pepper. Toss to coat evenly.
4. Place the seasoned vegetable mixture in the air fryer basket in an even layer.
5. Cook for 15-20 minutes, shaking the basket halfway through, until the potatoes are crispy and golden brown.
6. Once the potatoes are cooked, transfer them to a serving dish.
7. Sprinkle the crumbled feta cheese over the top.
8. Garnish with fresh parsley before serving.

 Prep time: 10 min

 Cook time: 20 min

 Servings: 2

Ingredients

- 2 large potatoes, diced
- 1 red bell pepper, diced
- 1 small red onion, finely chopped
- 2 cloves garlic, minced
- 1 tbsp olive oil
- 1 tsp dried oregano
- 1 tsp smoked paprika
- 1/2 tsp ground cumin
- Salt and pepper to taste
- 1/4 cup feta cheese, crumbled
- Fresh parsley for garnish

Smashed Egg Toasts with Herby Lemon Yogurt

Combining eggs with yogurt is a traditional practice in various Mediterranean and Middle Eastern cuisines. Greek yogurt adds a creamy, tangy flavor that complements the rich taste of the eggs. Fresh herbs and lemon zest brighten the dish, providing a refreshing contrast to the savory eggs. This simple yet flavorful breakfast option is not only nutritious but also showcases the Mediterranean diet's emphasis on fresh, wholesome ingredients. Cooking the eggs in an air fryer ensures they are perfectly done with minimal effort, making this a quick and easy meal for any time of day.

Nutrition Cal 280; Protein 18 g; Fat 14 g; Carb; 20 g

Instructions

1. Preheat your air fryer to 350°F (175°C).
2. Place the eggs in the air fryer basket and cook for 8-10 minutes for hard-boiled eggs. Adjust time according to your preference for egg doneness.
3. Once cooked, remove the eggs from the air fryer, cool slightly, then peel and set aside.
4. In a small bowl, combine the Greek yogurt, chopped parsley, dill, chives, lemon zest, lemon juice, salt, and pepper. Mix well.
5. Toast the whole grain bread slices in a toaster or in the air fryer for 2-3 minutes until golden and crisp.
6. Spread a generous layer of the herby lemon yogurt on each slice of toasted bread.
7. Place fresh arugula or spinach leaves on top of the yogurt.
8. Roughly chop or smash the cooked eggs and place them on top of the greens on each toast.
9. Drizzle a little olive oil over the eggs and season with additional salt and pepper if desired.
10. Serve the smashed egg toasts immediately while the toast is still warm.

 Prep time: 10 min

 Cook time: 10 min

 Servings: 2

Ingredients

- 4 large eggs
- 2 slices whole grain bread, toasted
- 1/2 cup Greek yogurt
- 1 tbsp fresh parsley, chopped
- 1 tbsp fresh dill, chopped
- 1 tbsp fresh chives, chopped
- 1 tsp lemon zest
- 1 tbsp lemon juice
- Salt and pepper to taste
- Olive oil spray
- Fresh arugula or spinach leaves for garnish

Chickpeas and Scrambled Eggs with Garlicky Greens and Yogurt

Chickpeas, also known as garbanzo beans, have been cultivated in Middle Eastern and Mediterranean regions for thousands of years and are a staple in dishes like hummus and falafel. They are rich in protein and fiber, making them an excellent addition to any meal. This dish combines the hearty crunch of air-fried chickpeas with the creaminess of scrambled eggs and the nutrition of garlicky greens. The spicy yogurt adds a zesty kick, showcasing the vibrant flavors of Mediterranean cuisine while providing a balanced and satisfying meal.

Nutrition Cal 350; Protein 20 g; Fat 20 g; Carb; 25 g

Instructions

1. Preheat your air fryer to 375°F (190°C).
2. In a bowl, toss the chickpeas with olive oil, smoked paprika, ground cumin, garlic powder, salt, and pepper.
3. Spread the chickpeas in an even layer in the air fryer basket.
4. Cook for 15-20 minutes, shaking the basket halfway through, until the chickpeas are crispy and golden brown.
5. In a small bowl, combine the Greek yogurt, harissa paste or hot sauce, lemon juice, and salt. Mix well and set aside.
6. In a large skillet, heat the olive oil over medium heat.
7. Add the minced garlic and sauté for about 1 minute until fragrant.
8. Add the chopped spinach or kale, salt, and pepper. Cook, stirring frequently, until the greens are wilted and tender, about 3-5 minutes. Remove from heat and set aside.
9. In a bowl, whisk together the eggs, milk or cream, salt, and pepper.
10. In the same skillet used for the greens, melt the butter or heat the olive oil over medium heat.
11. Pour the egg mixture into the skillet. Cook, stirring gently, until the eggs are softly scrambled and cooked to your desired consistency. Remove from heat.
12. Divide the crispy chickpeas, scrambled eggs, and garlicky greens between two plates.
13. Serve with a dollop of spicy yogurt on the side.

 Prep time: 10 min

 Cook time: 20 min

 Servings: 2

Ingredients

- 1 can (15 oz) chickpeas, drained and rinsed
- 3 tbsps olive oil
- 1 tsp smoked paprika
- 1/2 tsp ground cumin
- 1/2 tsp garlic powder
- 4 large eggs
- 1/4 cup milk or cream
- 2 cups fresh spinach or kale, chopped
- 2 cloves garlic, minced
- 1/2 cup Greek yogurt
- 1 tsp harissa paste or hot sauce (adjust to taste)
- 1 tbsp lemon juice
- Salt to taste

Zucchini and Parmesan Pancakes

Zucchini, a summer squash, is highly versatile and nutrient-dense, offering vitamins A and C, fiber, and antioxidants. The use of Parmesan cheese in these pancakes adds a savory depth of flavor and a crisp texture. Cooking them in an air fryer significantly reduces the amount of oil needed, making this dish a healthier alternative to traditional frying methods. These zucchini and Parmesan pancakes make for a delicious and nutritious breakfast, brunch, or side dish, embodying the principles of the Mediterranean diet with fresh, wholesome ingredients.

Nutrition Cal 250; Protein 14 g; Fat 12 g; Carb; 18 g

Instructions

1. Grate the zucchinis and place them in a colander. Sprinkle with a pinch of salt and let them sit for about 10 minutes to draw out excess moisture.
2. After 10 minutes, squeeze the grated zucchini in a clean kitchen towel or cheesecloth to remove as much liquid as possible.
3. In a large bowl, combine the grated zucchini, Parmesan cheese, flour, chopped green onions, beaten eggs, minced garlic, dried oregano, salt, and pepper. Mix until well combined.
4. Preheat your air fryer to 375°F (190°C).
5. Form the zucchini mixture into small patties, about 3 inches in diameter and 1/2 inch thick.
6. Lightly spray the air fryer basket with olive oil spray.
7. Place the zucchini pancakes in the air fryer basket in a single layer, leaving space between each pancake. You may need to cook them in batches depending on the size of your air fryer.
8. Air fry for 8-10 minutes, flipping halfway through, until the pancakes are golden brown and crispy on the outside.
9. Remove the pancakes from the air fryer and let them cool slightly before serving.
10. Serve warm with a dollop of Greek yogurt or tzatziki sauce on the side.

 Prep time: 15 min

 Cook time: 15 min

 Servings: 2

Ingredients

- 2 medium zucchinis, grated
- 1/2 cup grated Parmesan cheese
- 1/4 cup all-purpose flour (or almond flour for a gluten-free option)
- 1/4 cup finely chopped green onions
- 2 large eggs, lightly beaten
- 1 clove garlic, minced
- 1/2 tsp dried oregano
- Salt and pepper to taste
- Olive oil spray

BEEF, PORK AND LAMB

Greek-Style Pork Chops

Pork has been a significant part of Greek cuisine for centuries, often marinated with herbs and citrus to enhance its flavor. This recipe combines traditional Greek ingredients like olive oil, lemon, and oregano, which not only add delicious flavor but also offer health benefits typical of the Mediterranean diet. Air frying the pork chops ensures they are cooked to perfection with a crispy exterior and juicy interior, all while using less oil than traditional frying methods. The fresh topping of feta, tomatoes, and cucumbers adds a refreshing contrast and extra nutrients, making this dish both flavorful and nutritious.

Nutrition   Cal 350; Protein 28 g; Fat 24 g; Carb 4 g

Instructions

1. In a small bowl, combine the olive oil, minced garlic, lemon juice, lemon zest, dried oregano, dried thyme, salt, and pepper. Mix well.
2. Rub the marinade over the pork chops, ensuring they are well coated. Let them marinate for at least 10 minutes, or up to 1 hour for more flavor.
3. Preheat your air fryer to 375°F (190°C).
4. Place the marinated pork chops in the air fryer basket in a single layer.
5. Cook for 12-15 minutes, flipping halfway through, until the pork chops are golden brown and reach an internal temperature of 145°F (63°C).
6. While the pork chops are cooking, in a small bowl, combine the crumbled feta cheese, diced tomatoes, and diced cucumber.
7. Once the pork chops are cooked, remove them from the air fryer and let them rest for a few minutes.
8. Top each pork chop with the feta, tomato, and cucumber mixture.
9. Garnish with fresh parsley before serving.

 Prep time: 10 min

 Cook time: 15 min

 Servings: 2

Ingredients

- 2 boneless pork chops (about 1 inch thick)
- 2 tbsp olive oil
- 2 cloves garlic, minced
- 1 tbsp fresh lemon juice
- 1 tsp lemon zest
- 1 tsp dried oregano
- 1/2 tsp dried thyme
- Salt and pepper to taste
- 1/4 cup crumbled feta cheese
- 1/4 cup diced tomatoes
- 1/4 cup diced cucumber
- Fresh parsley for garnish

Mediterranean Style Pork Ribs

Pork ribs, traditionally enjoyed in various cuisines worldwide, take on a Mediterranean twist in this recipe with the use of herbs like oregano and thyme, and the bright flavor of lemon. These ingredients are staples in the Mediterranean diet, known for their health benefits and delicious flavors. Air frying the ribs not only reduces the cooking time compared to traditional methods but also requires less oil, resulting in a healthier yet equally flavorful dish. This method ensures the ribs are tender on the inside with a delightful crispy exterior.

Nutrition   Cal 450; Protein 30 g; Fat 35 g; Carb 2 g

Instructions

1. In a small bowl, combine the olive oil, minced garlic, lemon juice, lemon zest, dried oregano, dried thyme, smoked paprika, ground cumin, salt, and pepper. Mix well.
2. Remove the membrane from the back of the ribs for more tender meat.
3. Rub the marinade all over the ribs, ensuring they are well coated. Cover and refrigerate for at least 2 hours, or overnight for best results.
4. Preheat your air fryer to 375°F (190°C).
5. Cut the ribs into smaller sections to fit into the air fryer basket.
6. Place the ribs in the air fryer basket in a single layer.
7. Cook for 20-25 minutes, flipping halfway through, until the ribs are cooked through and have a nice char. The internal temperature should reach 145°F (63°C).
8. Once cooked, remove the ribs from the air fryer and let them rest for a few minutes.
9. Garnish with fresh parsley and serve with lemon wedges on the side.

 Prep time: 15 min

 Cook time: 25 min

 Servings: 2

Ingredients

- 1 rack of baby back pork ribs (about 1.5 lbs)
- 2 tbsp olive oil
- 3 cloves garlic, minced
- 2 tbsp lemon juice
- 1 tsp lemon zest
- 1 tbsp dried oregano
- 1 tsp dried thyme
- 1 tsp smoked paprika
- 1 tsp ground cumin
- Salt and pepper to taste
- Fresh parsley for garnish
- Lemon wedges for serving

Greek Pork Souvlaki

Souvlaki, a popular Greek street food, consists of marinated meat grilled on skewers and is often served with pita bread and various accompaniments. The word "souvlaki" means "skewer" in Greek. This dish captures the essence of Greek cuisine with its simple yet flavorful marinade and fresh ingredients. Using an air fryer to cook the souvlaki ensures the pork is tender and juicy with a delicious char, making it a healthier and more convenient alternative to traditional grilling methods.

Nutrition   Cal 400; Protein 30 g; Fat 20 g; Carb 20 g

Instructions

1. In a large bowl, combine the olive oil, minced garlic, lemon juice, lemon zest, red wine vinegar, dried oregano, dried thyme, smoked paprika, salt, and pepper. Mix well.
2. Add the pork cubes to the marinade, ensuring they are well coated. Cover and refrigerate for at least 2 hours, or overnight for best results.
3. Preheat your air fryer to 375°F (190°C).
4. 4.Assemble the Skewers:
5. Thread the marinated pork cubes onto the skewers, alternating with red onion wedges and bell pepper chunks.
6. Place the skewers in the air fryer basket in a single layer. You may need to cook them in batches depending on the size of your air fryer.
7. Cook for 12-15 minutes, turning halfway through, until the pork is cooked through and slightly charred. The internal temperature should reach 145°F (63°C).
8. Warm the pita bread in the air fryer for 1-2 minutes.
9. Serve the pork souvlaki on the warm pita bread with a generous dollop of tzatziki sauce, fresh chopped tomatoes, sliced red onions, and a sprinkle of fresh parsley.
10. Garnish with lemon wedges on the side.

 Prep time: 20 min

 Cook time: 15 min

 Servings: 2

Ingredients

- 1 lb pork tenderloin, cut into 1-inch cubes
- 2 tbsp olive oil
- 3 cloves garlic, minced
- 2 tbsp lemon juice
- 1 tsp lemon zest
- 1 tbsp red wine vinegar
- 1 tbsp dried oregano
- 1 tsp dried thyme
- 1 tsp smoked paprika
- Salt and pepper to taste
- 1 small red onion, cut into wedges
- 1 small bell pepper, cut into chunks
- Wooden or metal skewers (if using wooden, soak in water for 30 minutes)

Cheesy Topped Mediterranean Pork Loin Chops

Pork loin chops are a lean and tender cut of meat that can be easily enhanced with bold Mediterranean flavors. This recipe incorporates classic ingredients like sun-dried tomatoes, Kalamata olives, and feta cheese, which are staples in Mediterranean cuisine. The combination of these ingredients not only adds a burst of flavor but also provides a delightful contrast in texture. Air frying the pork chops ensures they are cooked evenly and quickly while maintaining their juiciness. The cheesy topping adds a rich and savory finish, making this dish a delicious and satisfying meal.

Nutrition   Cal 450; Protein 35 g; Fat 30 g; Carb 5 g

Instructions

1. In a small bowl, combine the olive oil, minced garlic, dried oregano, dried thyme, smoked paprika, salt, and pepper. Mix well.
2. Rub the mixture all over the pork loin chops, ensuring they are well coated.
3. Preheat your air fryer to 375°F (190°C).
4. Place the pork loin chops in the air fryer basket in a single layer.
5. Cook for 10 minutes, flipping halfway through.
6. After 10 minutes, open the air fryer and top each pork chop with the chopped sun-dried tomatoes, sliced Kalamata olives, crumbled feta cheese, and shredded mozzarella cheese.
7. Cook for an additional 5 minutes, or until the cheese is melted and bubbly and the pork reaches an internal temperature of 145°F (63°C).
8. Once cooked, remove the pork chops from the air fryer and let them rest for a few minutes.
9. Garnish with fresh parsley and serve with lemon wedges on the side.

 Prep time: 10 min

 Cook time: 15 min

 Servings: 2

Ingredients

- 2 boneless pork loin chops (about 1 inch thick)
- 2 tbsp olive oil
- 2 cloves garlic, minced
- 1 tsp dried oregano
- 1 tsp dried thyme
- 1 tsp smoked paprika
- Salt and pepper to taste
- 1/4 cup sun-dried tomatoes, chopped
- 1/4 cup Kalamata olives, sliced
- 1/2 cup feta cheese, crumbled
- 1/4 cup shredded mozzarella cheese
- Fresh parsley for garnish
- Lemon wedges for serving

Mediterranean Pork Tenderloin Crostini

Crostini, which means "little toasts" in Italian, are small pieces of toasted bread that are often topped with various ingredients to create a delicious appetizer or snack. This Mediterranean-inspired version features succulent pork tenderloin, which is marinated in classic Mediterranean flavors like lemon, garlic, and herbs. Paired with creamy hummus, tangy sun-dried tomatoes, salty Kalamata olives, and crumbled feta cheese, these crostini offer a delightful burst of flavors and textures. Air frying the pork and baguette slices ensures a quick and efficient cooking process, making this dish both convenient and impressive.

Nutrition   Cal 480; Protein 30 g; Fat 28 g; Carb 26 g

Instructions

1. In a small bowl, combine the olive oil, minced garlic, lemon juice, lemon zest, dried oregano, dried thyme, smoked paprika, salt, and pepper. Mix well.
2. Rub the marinade all over the pork tenderloin, ensuring it is well coated. Let it marinate for at least 15 minutes, or up to 1 hour for more flavor.
3. Preheat your air fryer to 375°F (190°C).
4. Place the marinated pork tenderloin in the air fryer basket.
5. Cook for 15-20 minutes, turning halfway through, until the pork reaches an internal temperature of 145°F (63°C).
6. Once cooked, remove the pork tenderloin from the air fryer and let it rest for a few minutes before slicing.
7. While the pork is resting, brush the baguette slices with olive oil and place them in the air fryer basket.
8. Toast the baguette slices at 350°F (175°C) for 3-5 minutes, or until they are golden and crispy.
9. Spread a generous amount of hummus on each toasted baguette slice.
10. Top with slices of the cooked pork tenderloin.
11. Add a few pieces of chopped sun-dried tomatoes and sliced Kalamata olives on top.
12. Sprinkle with crumbled feta cheese and garnish with fresh basil or parsley.
13. Arrange the crostini on a serving platter.
14. Serve immediately with lemon wedges on the side.

 Prep time: 15 min

 Cook time: 20 min

 Servings: 2

Ingredients

For the Pork Tenderloin:
- 1 pork tenderloin (about 1 lb)
- 2 tbsp olive oil
- 2 cloves garlic, minced
- 1 tbsp lemon juice
- 1 tsp lemon zest
- 1 tbsp dried oregano
- 1 tsp dried thyme
- 1 tsp smoked paprika
- Salt and pepper to taste

For the Crostini:
- 1 small baguette, sliced into 1/2 inch rounds
- 1/4 cup olive oil
- 1/2 cup hummus
- 1/4 cup sun-dried tomatoes, chopped
- 1/4 cup Kalamata olives, sliced
- 1/4 cup feta cheese, crumbled
- Fresh basil or parsley for garnish
- Lemon wedges for serving

Mediterranean Beef Patties

Mediterranean cuisine is renowned for its use of fresh herbs, vegetables, and bold flavors. These beef patties incorporate classic Mediterranean ingredients like Kalamata olives, sun-dried tomatoes, and feta cheese, which not only enhance the flavor but also add nutritional benefits. Air frying the patties reduces the amount of oil needed for cooking, making this dish a healthier alternative to traditional frying methods. These patties are versatile and can be enjoyed on their own, in a wrap, or as part of a larger Mediterranean-inspired meal.

Nutrition   Cal 400; Protein 28 g; Fat 28 g; Carb 8 g

Instructions

1. In a large bowl, combine the ground beef, finely chopped red onion, minced garlic, chopped parsley, chopped Kalamata olives, chopped sun-dried tomatoes, crumbled feta cheese, dried oregano, ground cumin, smoked paprika, salt, and pepper.
2. Add the lightly beaten egg and breadcrumbs (or almond flour). Mix well until all ingredients are evenly incorporated.
3. Divide the beef mixture into equal portions and shape them into patties, about 1/2 inch thick. This recipe should make about 4-6 patties, depending on size.
4. Preheat your air fryer to 375°F (190°C).
5. Lightly spray the air fryer basket with olive oil spray.
6. Place the patties in the air fryer basket in a single layer, ensuring they do not touch.
7. Cook for 12-15 minutes, flipping halfway through, until the patties are cooked to your desired level of doneness and have a nice crust on the outside.
8. Serve the Mediterranean beef patties on a plate with a side of Greek salad, pita bread, or in a pita wrap with tzatziki sauce, fresh lettuce, and tomato slices.

 Prep time: 15 min

 Cook time: 15 min

 Servings: 2

Ingredients

- 1 lb ground beef (preferably lean)
- 1/4 cup red onion, finely chopped
- 2 cloves garlic, minced
- 1/4 cup parsley, chopped
- 1/4 cup Kalamata olives, chopped
- 1/4 cup sun-dried tomatoes, chopped
- 1/4 cup feta cheese, crumbled
- 1 tsp dried oregano
- 1 tsp ground cumin
- 1/2 tsp smoked paprika
- Salt and pepper to taste
- 1 egg, lightly beaten
- 1/4 cup breadcrumbs (or almond flour for a gluten-free option)
- Olive oil spray

Beef and Feta Stuffed Zucchini

Stuffed vegetables are a traditional component of Mediterranean cuisine, enjoyed for their versatility and the ability to incorporate a variety of ingredients. Zucchini, a nutrient-dense summer squash, provides a perfect vessel for flavorful fillings like ground beef and feta cheese. This dish combines the savory richness of beef with the tangy creaminess of feta, balanced by the fresh flavors of herbs and tomatoes. Using an air fryer makes the cooking process quicker and healthier, preserving the nutrients and enhancing the natural flavors of the ingredients.

Nutrition Cal 350; Protein 25 g; Fat 22 g; Carb 12 g

Instructions

1. Cut the zucchinis in half lengthwise and scoop out the seeds and some flesh to create a hollow center for stuffing. Reserve the scooped-out flesh and chop it finely.
2. Preheat a skillet over medium heat and add the olive oil.
3. Add the chopped red onion and minced garlic to the skillet and sauté until fragrant and softened, about 2-3 minutes.
4. Add the ground beef to the skillet, breaking it up with a spoon, and cook until browned, about 5-7 minutes.
5. Stir in the chopped tomatoes, reserved zucchini flesh, Kalamata olives, dried oregano, salt, and pepper. Cook for another 3-4 minutes until the mixture is well combined and heated through.
6. Remove the skillet from heat and stir in the crumbled feta cheese, chopped parsley, and dill.
7. Preheat your air fryer to 375°F (190°C).
8. Spoon the beef and feta mixture into the hollowed-out zucchinis, packing the filling firmly.
9. Place the stuffed zucchinis in the air fryer basket in a single layer.
10. Air fry for 12-15 minutes until the zucchinis are tender and the filling is golden brown on top.
11. Carefully remove the stuffed zucchinis from the air fryer and let them cool for a few minutes.
12. Serve warm, garnished with additional chopped parsley and dill if desired.

 Prep time: 20 min

 Cook time: 15 min

 Servings: 2

Ingredients

- 2 medium zucchinis
- 1/2 lb ground beef (preferably lean)
- 1/4 cup red onion, finely chopped
- 2 cloves garlic, minced
- 1/2 cup tomatoes, chopped
- 1/4 cup Kalamata olives, chopped
- 1/4 cup feta cheese, crumbled
- 1 tbsp fresh parsley, chopped
- 1 tbsp fresh dill, chopped
- 1 tsp dried oregano
- Salt and pepper to taste
- 1 tbsp olive oil

Beef Kofta Kebabs

Kofta kebabs are a popular dish in Middle Eastern and Mediterranean cuisines, consisting of spiced ground meat shaped into kebabs and grilled. The word "kofta" comes from the Persian word for "pounded meat." These kebabs are known for their aromatic and flavorful blend of spices, which vary slightly depending on the region. Air frying the kofta kebabs ensures they are cooked evenly and quickly while retaining their juiciness. This method also provides a healthier alternative to traditional grilling, as it requires less oil and minimizes smoke and char.

Nutrition   Cal 420; Protein 28 g; Fat 28 g; Carb 8 g

Instructions

1. In a large bowl, combine the ground beef, finely chopped red onion, minced garlic, chopped parsley, chopped mint, ground cumin, ground coriander, smoked paprika, ground cinnamon, ground allspice, ground black pepper, and salt. Mix well until all ingredients are thoroughly incorporated.
2. Divide the mixture into equal portions and shape each portion around a skewer to form long, log-shaped kebabs. Ensure they are tightly packed to stay on the skewers.
3. Preheat your air fryer to 375°F (190°C).
4. Lightly spray the air fryer basket with olive oil spray.
5. Place the kofta kebabs in the air fryer basket in a single layer, ensuring they do not touch.
6. Cook for 12-15 minutes, turning halfway through, until the kebabs are browned and cooked through.
7. Serve the kofta kebabs with pita bread or flatbread, tzatziki sauce, sliced red onions, chopped tomatoes, and garnish with fresh parsley or mint.

 Prep time: 20 min

 Cook time: 15 min

 Servings: 2

Ingredients

- 1 lb ground beef (preferably lean)
- 1/4 cup red onion, finely chopped
- 2 cloves garlic, minced
- 1/4 cup fresh parsley, chopped
- 1/4 cup fresh mint, chopped
- 1 tsp ground cumin
- 1 tsp ground coriander
- 1 tsp smoked paprika
- 1/2 tsp ground cinnamon
- 1/2 tsp ground allspice
- 1/2 tsp ground black pepper
- 1 tsp salt
- Olive oil spray
- Wooden or metal skewers.

Steak Bites with Yogurt Sauce

Steak bites are a versatile and flavorful way to enjoy beef, and when combined with Mediterranean spices and herbs, they become even more delicious. The yogurt sauce adds a refreshing and tangy element, typical of Mediterranean cuisine, which often incorporates yogurt in savory dishes. Air frying the steak bites ensures they are crispy on the outside and juicy on the inside, all while using less oil and cooking in a fraction of the time compared to traditional methods. This dish is perfect for a quick and healthy dinner that doesn't compromise on flavor.

Nutrition   Cal 450; Protein 35 g; Fat 30 g; Carb 5 g

Instructions

1. In a bowl, combine the olive oil, minced garlic, dried oregano, dried thyme, smoked paprika, salt, and pepper. Mix well.
2. Add the steak pieces to the bowl and toss to coat evenly. Let them marinate for at least 15 minutes.
3. Preheat your air fryer to 400°F (200°C).
4. Place the marinated steak bites in the air fryer basket in a single layer.
5. Cook for 8-10 minutes, shaking the basket halfway through, until the steak bites are browned and cooked to your desired level of doneness.
6. While the steak is cooking, in a small bowl, combine the Greek yogurt, lemon juice, lemon zest, minced garlic, chopped dill, salt, and pepper. Mix well and set aside.
7. Once the steak bites are cooked, remove them from the air fryer and let them rest for a few minutes.
8. Serve the steak bites on a plate, garnished with fresh parsley.
9. Serve with the yogurt sauce on the side for dipping.

 Prep time: 15 min

 Cook time: 10 min

 Servings: 2

Ingredients

- 1 lb steak (such as sirloin or ribeye), cut into bite-sized pieces
- 2 tbsp olive oil
- 2 cloves garlic, minced
- 1 tsp dried oregano
- 1 tsp dried thyme
- 1 tsp smoked paprika
- Salt and pepper to taste
- Fresh parsley for garnish

For the Yogurt Sauce:
- 1/2 cup Greek yogurt
- 1 tbsp lemon juice
- 1 tsp lemon zest
- 1 clove garlic, minced
- 1 tbsp fresh dill, chopped
- Salt and pepper to taste

Steak Bowls

Mediterranean cuisine is known for its balanced and wholesome ingredients, often incorporating fresh vegetables, lean proteins, and healthy fats. This Mediterranean steak bowl is a perfect example of this approach, combining flavorful marinated steak with a variety of fresh vegetables and a refreshing yogurt sauce. Quinoa or couscous serves as a nutritious base, providing a good source of protein and fiber. Air frying the steak bites ensures they are cooked quickly and evenly, making this dish not only delicious but also convenient for a healthy weeknight meal.

Nutrition Cal 500; Protein 35 g; Fat 28 g; Carb 25 g

Instructions

1. In a bowl, combine the olive oil, minced garlic, dried oregano, dried thyme, smoked paprika, salt, and pepper. Mix well.
2. Add the steak pieces to the bowl and toss to coat evenly. Let them marinate for at least 15 minutes.
3. Preheat your air fryer to 400°F (200°C).
4. Place the marinated steak bites in the air fryer basket in a single layer.
5. Cook for 8-10 minutes, shaking the basket halfway through, until the steak bites are browned and cooked to your desired level of doneness.
6. While the steak is cooking, in a small bowl, combine the Greek yogurt, lemon juice, lemon zest, minced garlic, chopped dill, salt, and pepper. Mix well and set aside.
7. Divide the cooked quinoa or couscous between two bowls.
8. Arrange the cherry tomatoes, diced cucumber, red onion, Kalamata olives, and feta cheese around the bowl.
9. Add the cooked steak bites on top.
10. Drizzle with the yogurt sauce.
11. Garnish with fresh parsley.
12. Serve immediately, with extra yogurt sauce on the side if desired.

 Prep time: 20 min

 Cook time: 15 min

 Servings: 2

Ingredients

- 1 lb steak (such as sirloin or ribeye), cut into bite-sized pieces
- 2 tbsp olive oil
- 2 cloves garlic, minced
- 1 tsp dried oregano
- 1 tsp dried thyme
- 1 tsp smoked paprika
- Salt and pepper to taste

For the Bowls:
- 1 cup cooked quinoa or couscous
- 1 cup cherry tomatoes, halved
- 1 cucumber, diced
- 1/4 cup red onion, finely chopped
- 1/4 cup Kalamata olives, sliced
- 1/4 cup feta cheese, crumbled
- Fresh parsley, chopped

For the Yogurt Sauce:
- 1/2 cup Greek yogurt
- 1 tbsp lemon juice
- 1 tsp lemon zest
- 1 clove garlic, minced
- 1 tbsp fresh dill, chopped
- Salt and pepper to taste

Beef Meatballs

Meatballs are a beloved dish in many cultures, and the Mediterranean version is no exception. These beef meatballs are infused with classic Mediterranean flavors from ingredients like Kalamata olives, feta cheese, and fresh herbs. The combination of spices such as cumin and cinnamon adds a unique depth of flavor. Air frying the meatballs ensures they are cooked evenly and quickly with minimal added fat, making this dish a healthier alternative to traditional frying methods. Served with fresh vegetables and a tangy tzatziki sauce, these meatballs make for a delicious and balanced meal.

Nutrition   Cal 450; Protein 30 g; Fat 28 g; Carb 12 g

Instructions

1. chopped parsley, chopped mint, chopped Kalamata olives, crumbled feta cheese, dried oregano, ground cumin, ground cinnamon, ground black pepper, and salt.
2. Add the lightly beaten egg and breadcrumbs (or almond flour). Mix well until all ingredients are thoroughly incorporated.
3. Divide the mixture into equal portions and shape each portion into meatballs, about 1 inch in diameter. This recipe should make about 16-20 meatballs, depending on size.
4. Preheat your air fryer to 375°F (190°C).
5. Lightly spray the air fryer basket with olive oil spray.
6. Place the meatballs in the air fryer basket in a single layer, ensuring they do not touch.
7. Cook for 12-15 minutes, shaking the basket halfway through, until the meatballs are browned and cooked through.
8. Serve the meatballs with pita bread or flatbread, tzatziki sauce, sliced red onions, chopped tomatoes, and garnish with fresh parsley or mint.

 Prep time: 20 min

 Cook time: 15 min

 Servings: 2

Ingredients

- 1 lb ground beef (preferably lean)
- 1/4 cup red onion, finely chopped
- 2 cloves garlic, minced
- 1/4 cup fresh parsley, chopped
- 1/4 cup fresh mint, chopped
- 1/4 cup Kalamata olives, chopped
- 1/4 cup feta cheese, crumbled
- 1 tsp dried oregano
- 1 tsp ground cumin
- 1/2 tsp ground cinnamon
- 1/2 tsp ground black pepper
- 1 tsp salt
- 1 egg, lightly beaten
- 1/4 cup breadcrumbs (or almond flour for a gluten-free option)
- Olive oil spray

Beef Chops Stuffed with Spinach and Feta

Stuffing meat with flavorful ingredients is a technique used in various cuisines to add moisture and enhance the flavor. In this Mediterranean-inspired dish, the combination of spinach and feta cheese provides a nutritious and delicious filling that complements the rich taste of the beef. Spinach is packed with vitamins and minerals, while feta adds a tangy and creamy texture. Air frying the beef chops ensures they are cooked evenly and quickly, resulting in a tender and juicy dish with a crispy exterior.

Nutrition
Cal 500; Protein 40 g; Fat 32 g; Carb 6 g

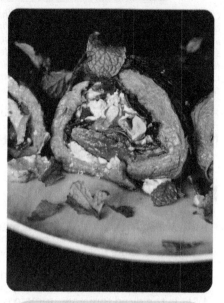

Instructions

1. In a skillet, heat the olive oil over medium heat.
2. Add the finely chopped red onion and minced garlic, and sauté until fragrant and softened, about 2-3 minutes.
3. Add the chopped spinach and cook until wilted, about 2-3 minutes.
4. Remove the skillet from heat and stir in the crumbled feta cheese, dried oregano, dried thyme, salt, and pepper. Mix well and let it cool slightly.
5. Using a sharp knife, make a horizontal slit in each beef chop to create a pocket for the stuffing. Be careful not to cut all the way through.
6. Spoon the spinach and feta mixture into the pocket of each beef chop, packing it firmly.
7. Secure the opening with toothpicks or kitchen twine to keep the stuffing inside.
8. Preheat your air fryer to 375°F (190°C).
9. Lightly spray the air fryer basket with olive oil spray.
10. Place the stuffed beef chops in the air fryer basket in a single layer.
11. Cook for 15-20 minutes, flipping halfway through, until the beef is cooked to your desired level of doneness and has a nice crust on the outside. The internal temperature should reach at least 145°F (63°C) for medium-rare.
12. Once cooked, remove the beef chops from the air fryer and let them rest for a few minutes.
13. Carefully remove the toothpicks or kitchen twine before serving.
14. Serve with a side of roasted vegetables or a fresh salad.

 Prep time: 20 min

 Cook time: 20 min

 Servings: 2

Ingredients

- 2 large beef chops (about 1 inch thick)
- 2 cups fresh spinach, chopped
- 1/2 cup feta cheese, crumbled
- 1/4 cup red onion, finely chopped
- 2 cloves garlic, minced
- 1 tbsp olive oil
- 1 tsp dried oregano
- 1 tsp dried thyme
- Salt and pepper to taste
- Toothpicks or kitchen twine

Beef Lasagna

Lasagna, a beloved Italian dish, is made healthier and more aligned with the Mediterranean diet in this recipe by incorporating ingredients like lean ground beef, Kalamata olives, sun-dried tomatoes, and a mix of ricotta and feta cheeses. Air frying the lasagna not only reduces the cooking time but also creates a perfectly crispy top layer while keeping the inside tender and flavorful. This Mediterranean twist on a classic lasagna makes for a delicious and nutritious meal that highlights the rich flavors and health benefits of Mediterranean cuisine.

Nutrition   Cal 550; Protein 35 g; Fat 30 g; Carb 35 g

Instructions

1. In a skillet, heat the olive oil over medium heat.
2. Add the finely chopped red onion and minced garlic, and sauté until fragrant and softened, about 2-3 minutes.
3. Add the ground beef and cook until browned, breaking it up with a spoon, about 5-7 minutes.
4. Stir in the diced tomatoes, tomato paste, Kalamata olives, sun-dried tomatoes, dried oregano, dried basil, ground cinnamon, salt, and pepper. Simmer for 10-15 minutes until the sauce thickens.
5. In a bowl, combine the ricotta cheese, crumbled feta cheese, chopped parsley, and the lightly beaten egg. Mix well.
6. Cook the lasagna noodles according to the package instructions until al dente. Drain and set aside.
7. Preheat your air fryer to 320°F (160°C).
8. In a small oven-safe dish or air fryer baking pan that fits into your air fryer basket, spread a thin layer of the meat sauce on the bottom.
9. Place a layer of lasagna noodles on top of the sauce, cutting them to fit if necessary.
10. Spread a layer of the cheese mixture over the noodles, followed by a layer of the meat sauce.
11. Repeat the layers until all ingredients are used, finishing with a layer of meat sauce.
12. Sprinkle the shredded mozzarella cheese on top.
13. Place the assembled lasagna in the air fryer basket.
14. Cook for 20-25 minutes until the cheese is melted and bubbly and the lasagna is heated through.
15. If the top browns too quickly, cover it with aluminum foil and continue cooking.
16. Once cooked, remove the lasagna from the air fryer and let it rest for a few minutes before slicing.
17. Garnish with fresh basil and serve.

 Prep time: 30 min

 Cook time: 40 min

 Servings: 2

Ingredients

- 1 lb ground beef (preferably lean)
- 1/2 cup red onion, finely chopped
- 2 cloves garlic, minced
- 1 can (14.5 oz) diced tomatoes
- 1/4 cup tomato paste
- 1/4 cup Kalamata olives, sliced
- 1/4 cup sun-dried tomatoes, chopped
- 1 tsp dried oregano
- 1 tsp dried basil
- 1/2 tsp ground cinnamon
- Salt and pepper to taste
- 1 tbsp olive oil

For the Cheese Mixture:
- 1 cup ricotta cheese
- 1/2 cup feta cheese, crumbled
- 1/4 cup fresh parsley, chopped
- 1 egg, lightly beaten

For the Lasagna:
- 6 lasagna noodles (preferably whole wheat or gluten-free)
- 1 cup shredded mozzarella cheese
- Fresh basil for garnish

Lamb Chops with Rosemary

Lamb is a staple in Mediterranean cuisine and is often paired with fresh herbs like rosemary and thyme, which grow abundantly in the region. Rosemary has been used since ancient times not only for its flavor but also for its potential health benefits, including improving digestion and circulation. Air frying lamb chops is a quick and efficient method that ensures a juicy, tender result with a crispy exterior. The addition of lemon zest in the marinade enhances the flavors and provides a refreshing citrus note that complements the richness of the lamb.

Nutrition   Cal 450; Protein 35 g; Fat 30 g; Carb 2 g

Instructions

1. In a small bowl, combine the olive oil, minced garlic, chopped rosemary, chopped thyme, lemon zest, salt, and pepper. Mix well.
2. Rub the marinade all over the lamb chops, ensuring they are well coated.
3. Let the lamb chops marinate for at least 15 minutes, or up to 1 hour for more flavor.
4. Preheat your air fryer to 375°F (190°C).
5. Place the marinated lamb chops in the air fryer basket in a single layer.
6. Cook for 12-15 minutes, flipping halfway through, until the lamb chops reach your desired level of doneness. For medium-rare, aim for an internal temperature of 145°F (63°C).
7. Once cooked, remove the lamb chops from the air fryer and let them rest for 5 minutes to allow the juices to redistribute.
8. Serve the lamb chops with lemon wedges on the side.

 Prep time: 30 min

 Cook time: 40 min

 Servings: 2

Ingredients

- 4 lamb chops (about 1 inch thick)
- 2 tbsp olive oil
- 3 cloves garlic, minced
- 1 tbsp fresh rosemary, chopped (or 1 tsp dried rosemary)
- 1 tsp fresh thyme, chopped (or 1/2 tsp dried thyme)
- 1 tsp lemon zest
- Salt and pepper to taste
- Lemon wedges for serving

Lamb Gyros

Gyros, a popular Greek street food, are typically made with meat cooked on a vertical rotisserie. The word "gyro" means "turn" in Greek, referring to the rotating cooking method. This air-fried version captures the traditional flavors with a convenient and healthier cooking method. The combination of marinated lamb, fresh vegetables, and creamy tzatziki sauce wrapped in soft pita bread creates a delicious and satisfying meal that embodies the essence of Mediterranean cuisine.

Nutrition Cal 600; Protein 40 g; Fat 35 g; Carb 30 g

Instructions

1. In a small bowl, combine the olive oil, minced garlic, chopped rosemary, chopped thyme, lemon zest, salt, and pepper. Mix well.
2. Rub the marinade all over the lamb chops, ensuring they are well coated.
3. Let the lamb chops marinate for at least 15 minutes, or up to 1 hour for more flavor.
4. Preheat your air fryer to 375°F (190°C).
5. Place the marinated lamb chops in the air fryer basket in a single layer.
6. Cook for 12-15 minutes, flipping halfway through, until the lamb chops reach your desired level of doneness. For medium-rare, aim for an internal temperature of 145°F (63°C).
7. Once cooked, remove the lamb chops from the air fryer and let them rest for 5 minutes to allow the juices to redistribute.
8. Serve the lamb chops with lemon wedges on the side.

 Prep time: 30 min

 Cook time: 40 min

 Servings: 2

Ingredients
- 1 lb lamb shoulder or leg, cut into thin strips
- 2 tbsp olive oil
- 3 cloves garlic, minced
- 1 tbsp fresh lemon juice
- 1 tsp lemon zest
- 1 tbsp dried oregano
- 1 tsp ground cumin
- 1 tsp smoked paprika
- 1/2 tsp ground coriander
- Salt and pepper to taste

For the Tzatziki Sauce:
- 1/2 cup Greek yogurt
- 1/2 cucumber, grated and excess water squeezed out
- 1 clove garlic, minced
- 1 tbsp fresh dill, chopped
- 1 tbsp fresh lemon juice
- Salt and pepper to taste

For Serving:
- 2 pita breads or flatbreads
- 1/2 cup cherry tomatoes, halved
- 1/4 cup red onion, thinly sliced
- 1/4 cup Kalamata olives, sliced
- Fresh parsley or mint for garnish
- Lemon wedges

Lamb and Pine Nut Mini Pies

Mini meat pies, known as "empanadas" in Spanish or "sfiha" in Middle Eastern cuisine, are a popular snack or appetizer in many cultures. The combination of lamb and pine nuts in this recipe reflects traditional Middle Eastern flavors, where pine nuts are often used to add a rich, nutty taste to meat dishes. Air frying these mini pies provides a healthier alternative to deep frying, ensuring they are crispy on the outside while maintaining a juicy and flavorful filling. These lamb and pine nut mini pies are perfect for a party appetizer or a satisfying snack.

Nutrition Cal 450; Protein 25 g; Fat 30 g; Carb 20 g

Instructions

1. In a skillet, heat the olive oil over medium heat.
2. Add the finely chopped red onion and minced garlic, and sauté until fragrant and softened, about 2-3 minutes.
3. Add the ground lamb to the skillet and cook until browned, breaking it up with a spoon, about 5-7 minutes.
4. Stir in the pine nuts, ground cumin, ground cinnamon, ground allspice, salt, and pepper. Cook for another 2-3 minutes until the mixture is well combined.
5. Remove the skillet from heat and stir in the chopped parsley. Let the filling cool slightly.
6. In a large bowl, combine the flour and salt. Make a well in the center and add the olive oil and warm water.
7. Mix until a dough forms, then knead on a floured surface for about 5 minutes until smooth and elastic.
8. Divide the dough into 8 equal portions and roll each portion into a ball.
9. Preheat your air fryer to 375°F (190°C).
10. On a floured surface, roll out each dough ball into a small circle, about 4 inches in diameter.
11. Place a generous spoonful of the lamb filling in the center of each circle.
12. Fold the dough over the filling to form a half-moon shape and press the edges to seal. You can crimp the edges with a fork for a decorative touch.
13. Lightly spray the mini pies with olive oil spray.
14. Place the mini pies in the air fryer basket in a single layer. You may need to cook them in batches depending on the size of your air fryer.
15. Cook for 12-15 minutes until the pies are golden brown and crispy.
16. Once cooked, remove the mini pies from the air fryer and let them cool for a few minutes.
17. Garnish with fresh mint or parsley and serve with lemon wedges on the side.

 Prep time: 30 min

 Cook time: 20 min

 Servings: 2

Ingredients

For the Filling:
- 1 lb ground lamb
- 1/4 cup pine nuts
- 1/2 cup red onion, finely chopped
- 2 cloves garlic, minced
- 1/4 cup fresh parsley, chopped
- 1 tsp ground cumin
- 1 tsp ground cinnamon
- 1/2 tsp ground allspice
- Salt and pepper to taste
- 1 tbsp olive oil

For the Dough:
- 1 1/2 cups all-purpose flour (or use whole wheat flour for a healthier option)
- 1/2 tsp salt
- 1/4 cup olive oil
- 1/2 cup warm water

Lamb Stuffed Eggplant

Stuffed vegetables are a cornerstone of Mediterranean and Middle Eastern cuisines, offering a nutritious and flavorful way to enjoy seasonal produce. This dish combines the hearty taste of ground lamb with the nutty flavor of pine nuts and the sweet-tartness of sun-dried tomatoes. The use of aromatic spices like cumin, cinnamon, and allspice adds depth and warmth to the filling. Air frying the eggplant not only speeds up the cooking process but also enhances its natural flavors, making this dish a delicious and healthy option for a satisfying meal.

Nutrition   Cal 450; Protein 25 g; Fat 30 g; Carb 20 g

Instructions

1. Preheat your air fryer to 375°F (190°C).
2. Cut the eggplant in half lengthwise and scoop out some of the flesh to create a hollow for the filling, leaving about a 1/2-inch border. Chop the scooped-out flesh and set aside.
3. Brush the inside of the eggplant halves with 1 tbsp olive oil and season with salt and pepper.
4. Place the eggplant halves in the air fryer basket, cut side up, and cook for 10 minutes until slightly softened.
5. In a skillet, heat 1 tbsp olive oil over medium heat.
6. Add the finely chopped red onion and minced garlic, and sauté until fragrant and softened, about 2-3 minutes.
7. Add the ground lamb to the skillet and cook until browned, breaking it up with a spoon, about 5-7 minutes.
8. Stir in the chopped eggplant flesh, pine nuts, sun-dried tomatoes, ground cumin, ground cinnamon, ground allspice, salt, and pepper. Cook for another 5 minutes until the mixture is well combined and the eggplant is tender.
9. Remove the skillet from heat and stir in the chopped parsley.
10. Spoon the lamb mixture into the hollowed-out eggplant halves, packing it firmly.
11. Return the stuffed eggplant halves to the air fryer basket.
12. Cook for an additional 15-20 minutes until the eggplant is tender and the filling is heated through.
13. Sprinkle the crumbled feta cheese over the top of the stuffed eggplant halves.
14. Air fry for an additional 2-3 minutes until the cheese is slightly melted.
15. Garnish with fresh mint or parsley before serving.

 Prep time: 20 min

 Cook time: 30 min

 Servings: 2

Ingredients

- o 1 large eggplant
- o 2 tbsp olive oil
- o Salt and pepper to taste

For the Filling:
- o 1/2 lb ground lamb
- o 1/4 cup red onion, finely chopped
- o 2 cloves garlic, minced
- o 1/4 cup pine nuts
- o 1/4 cup sun-dried tomatoes, chopped
- o 1 tsp ground cumin
- o 1 tsp ground cinnamon
- o 1/2 tsp ground allspice
- o Salt and pepper to taste
- o 1/4 cup fresh parsley, chopped
- o 1 tbsp olive oil

For Topping:
- o 1/4 cup feta cheese, crumbled
-   2 tbsp fresh mint or parsley, chopped

Spiced Lamb Ribs

Lamb ribs, often overlooked compared to lamb chops, offer a rich and flavorful eating experience, especially when spiced with a blend of aromatic Mediterranean spices. The combination of cumin, paprika, coriander, and cinnamon gives these ribs a warm and complex flavor profile, while the lemon adds a refreshing brightness. Air frying the ribs ensures they cook evenly and quickly, achieving a tender interior with a crispy exterior. This method also reduces the amount of added fat compared to traditional frying, making for a healthier yet still indulgent dish.

Nutrition   Cal 550; Protein 30 g; Fat 45 g; Carb 5 g

Instructions

1. In a small bowl, combine the olive oil, minced garlic, lemon juice, lemon zest, ground cumin, smoked paprika, ground coriander, ground cinnamon, ground allspice, dried oregano, salt, and pepper. Mix well.
2. Rub the marinade all over the lamb ribs, ensuring they are well coated. Let them marinate for at least 30 minutes, or up to 2 hours for more flavor.
3. Preheat your air fryer to 375°F (190°C).
4. Cut the rack of lamb ribs into individual ribs or smaller sections that fit into your air fryer basket.
5. Place the ribs in the air fryer basket in a single layer.
6. Cook for 20-25 minutes, flipping halfway through, until the ribs are cooked through and have a nice char. The internal temperature should reach at least 145°F (63°C) for medium-rare.
7. Once cooked, remove the lamb ribs from the air fryer and let them rest for 5 minutes to allow the juices to redistribute.
8. Garnish the lamb ribs with fresh parsley.
9. Serve with lemon wedges on the side.

 Prep time: 15 min

 Cook time: 25 min

 Servings: 2

Ingredients

- o 1 rack of lamb ribs (about 1.5 lbs)
- o 2 tbsp olive oil
- o 3 cloves garlic, minced
- o 1 tbsp fresh lemon juice
- o 1 tsp lemon zest
- o 1 tbsp ground cumin
- o 1 tbsp smoked paprika
- o 1 tsp ground coriander
- o 1 tsp ground cinnamon
- o 1 tsp ground allspice
- o 1 tsp dried oregano
- o Salt and pepper to taste
- o Fresh parsley for garnish
- o Lemon wedges for serving

Mediterranean Vegetables with Lamb

Lamb ribs, often overlooked compared to lamb chops, offer a rich and flavorful eating experience, especially when spiced with a blend of aromatic Mediterranean spices. The combination of cumin, paprika, coriander, and cinnamon gives these ribs a warm and complex flavor profile, while the lemon adds a refreshing brightness. Air frying the ribs ensures they cook evenly and quickly, achieving a tender interior with a crispy exterior. This method also reduces the amount of added fat compared to traditional frying, making for a healthier yet still indulgent dish.

Nutrition   Cal 500; Protein 35 g; Fat 30 g; Carb 20 g

Instructions

1. In a large bowl, combine the olive oil, minced garlic, lemon juice, lemon zest, dried oregano, ground cumin, smoked paprika, salt, and pepper. Mix well.
2. Add the lamb pieces to the bowl and toss to coat evenly. Let them marinate for at least 15 minutes.
3. Preheat your air fryer to 375°F (190°C).
4. In another large bowl, combine the zucchini, red bell pepper, yellow bell pepper, red onion, cherry tomatoes, and Kalamata olives.
5. Drizzle with olive oil and sprinkle with dried oregano, dried thyme, salt, and pepper. Toss to coat evenly.
6. Place the marinated lamb pieces in the air fryer basket in a single layer. Cook for 10-12 minutes, shaking the basket halfway through, until the lamb is browned and cooked through. Remove the lamb from the air fryer and set aside.
7. Add the prepared vegetables to the air fryer basket and cook for 12-15 minutes, shaking the basket halfway through, until the vegetables are tender and slightly charred.
8. Once the vegetables are cooked, return the lamb to the air fryer basket with the vegetables and cook for an additional 2-3 minutes to heat everything through.
9. Transfer the lamb and vegetables to a serving platter.
10. Garnish with fresh parsley and serve with lemon wedges on the side.

 Prep time: 15 min

 Cook time: 25 min

 Servings: 2

Ingredients

For the Lamb:
- 1 lb lamb shoulder or leg, cut into bite-sized pieces
- 2 tbsp olive oil
- 2 cloves garlic, minced
- 1 tbsp fresh lemon juice
- 1 tsp lemon zest
- 1 tbsp dried oregano
- 1 tsp ground cumin
- 1 tsp smoked paprika
- Salt and pepper to taste

For the Vegetables:
- 1 zucchini, sliced
- 1 red bell pepper, chopped
- 1 yellow bell pepper, chopped
- 1 red onion, chopped
- 1 cup cherry tomatoes
- 1/2 cup Kalamata olives, pitted and halved
- 1 tbsp olive oil
- 1 tsp dried oregano
- 1 tsp dried thyme
- Salt and pepper to taste

Greek Lamb Pie

Greek pies, known as "pites," are a traditional part of Greek cuisine and come in various forms, from savory to sweet. This Greek Lamb Pie combines the rich flavors of lamb with classic Mediterranean ingredients like spinach, sun-dried tomatoes, and Kalamata olives. The combination of spices such as cumin and cinnamon adds a warm depth of flavor, while feta cheese provides a tangy finish. Cooking the pie in an air fryer ensures a perfectly crispy crust with a juicy, flavorful filling, making this dish a delightful centerpiece for any meal.

Nutrition   Cal 600; Protein 30 g; Fat 40 g; Carb 30 g

Instructions

1. In a skillet, heat the olive oil over medium heat.
2. Add the finely chopped red onion and minced garlic, and sauté until fragrant and softened, about 2-3 minutes.
3. Add the ground lamb to the skillet and cook until browned, breaking it up with a spoon, about 5-7 minutes.
4. Stir in the chopped spinach, sun-dried tomatoes, Kalamata olives, dried oregano, ground cumin, ground cinnamon, salt, and pepper. Cook for another 3-4 minutes until the mixture is well combined and the spinach is wilted.
5. Remove the skillet from heat and stir in the crumbled feta cheese. Let the filling cool slightly.
6. In a large bowl, combine the flour and salt. Make a well in the center and add the olive oil and cold water.
7. Mix until a dough forms, then knead on a floured surface for about 5 minutes until smooth and elastic.
8. Divide the dough into two equal portions, one for the base and one for the top.
9. Preheat your air fryer to 350°F (175°C).
10. Roll out one portion of the dough into a circle large enough to fit the base and sides of your air fryer baking dish.
11. Place the rolled-out dough into the baking dish, pressing it into the corners.
12. Fill with the lamb mixture, spreading it evenly.
13. Roll out the second portion of the dough and place it over the filling. Trim any excess dough and crimp the edges to seal.
14. Brush the top with the beaten egg for a golden finish.
15. Place the assembled pie in the air fryer basket.
16. Cook for 30-35 minutes, until the crust is golden brown and crisp.
17. Once cooked, remove the pie from the air fryer and let it cool for a few minutes.
18. Garnish with fresh parsley before slicing and serving.

 Prep time: 15 min

 Cook time: 25 min

 Servings: 2

Ingredients

For the Filling:
- 1 lb ground lamb
- 1/2 cup red onion, finely chopped
- 3 cloves garlic, minced
- 1/2 cup spinach, chopped
- 1/4 cup sun-dried tomatoes, chopped
- 1/4 cup Kalamata olives, pitted and chopped
- 1 tsp dried oregano
- 1 tsp ground cumin
- 1/2 tsp ground cinnamon
- Salt and pepper to taste
- 1 tbsp olive oil
- 1/2 cup feta cheese, crumbled

For the Crust:
- 1 cup all-purpose flour (or whole wheat flour for a healthier option)
- 1/2 tsp salt
- 1/4 cup olive oil
- 1/4 cup cold water

For Assembly:
- 1 egg, lightly beaten (for egg wash)
  - Fresh parsley for garnish

CHICKEN AND TURKEY

Mediterranean Herb Chicken

The Mediterranean diet is renowned for its health benefits, including heart health and longevity, largely due to its emphasis on fresh herbs, olive oil, and lean proteins. This Mediterranean Herb Chicken recipe encapsulates these principles, using a flavorful marinade that highlights the aromatic herbs and citrus notes typical of the region. Air frying the chicken not only reduces the amount of added fat but also ensures the meat remains juicy and tender, making this dish a healthy and delicious option for any meal.

Nutrition   Cal 350; Protein 30 g; Fat 20 g; Carb 35 g

Instructions

1. In a small bowl, combine the olive oil, minced garlic, lemon juice, lemon zest, chopped rosemary, chopped thyme, dried oregano, salt, and pepper. Mix well.
2. Place the chicken breasts in a resealable plastic bag or a shallow dish.
3. Pour the marinade over the chicken, ensuring it is well coated. Seal the bag or cover the dish and let the chicken marinate in the refrigerator for at least 30 minutes, or up to 2 hours for more flavor.
4. Preheat your air fryer to 375°F (190°C).
5. Remove the chicken breasts from the marinade and place them in the air fryer basket in a single layer.
6. Cook for 18-20 minutes, flipping halfway through, until the chicken is cooked through and reaches an internal temperature of 165°F (74°C).
7. Once cooked, remove the chicken from the air fryer and let it rest for 5 minutes to allow the juices to redistribute.
8. Slice the chicken breasts and arrange them on a serving plate.
9. Garnish with fresh parsley and serve with lemon wedges on the side.

 Prep time: 15 min

 Cook time: 20 min

 Servings: 2

Ingredients

- 2 boneless, skinless chicken breasts
- 2 tbsp olive oil
- 3 cloves garlic, minced
- 1 tbsp fresh lemon juice
- 1 tsp lemon zest
- 1 tbsp fresh rosemary, chopped (or 1 tsp dried rosemary)
- 1 tbsp fresh thyme, chopped (or 1 tsp dried thyme)
- 1 tsp dried oregano
- Salt and pepper to taste
- Fresh parsley for garnish
- Lemon wedges for serving

Shawarma-Style Chicken

Shawarma is a popular Middle Eastern street food known for its flavorful, marinated meat that is traditionally cooked on a vertical rotisserie. This shawarma-style chicken recipe captures the essence of traditional shawarma by using a blend of aromatic spices that are characteristic of Middle Eastern cuisine. Air frying the chicken not only makes the cooking process quicker and healthier but also ensures that the meat remains juicy and tender. Serving the chicken with fresh vegetables and a tangy sauce in pita bread creates a delicious and satisfying meal that brings the flavors of the Middle East to your kitchen.

Nutrition Cal 450; Protein 30 g; Fat 25 g; Carb 30 g

Instructions

1. In a large bowl, combine the olive oil, minced garlic, lemon juice, lemon zest, ground cumin, ground coriander, ground paprika, ground turmeric, ground cinnamon, ground allspice, cayenne pepper (if using), salt, and pepper. Mix well.
2. Add the chicken breasts (or thighs) and sliced red onion to the bowl, tossing to coat evenly with the marinade.
3. Cover and refrigerate for at least 1 hour, or up to overnight for maximum flavor.
4. Preheat your air fryer to 375°F (190°C).
5. Place the marinated chicken and red onion slices in the air fryer basket in a single layer.
6. Cook for 18-20 minutes, flipping halfway through, until the chicken is cooked through and reaches an internal temperature of 165°F (74°C).
7. Once cooked, remove the chicken from the air fryer and let it rest for 5 minutes.
8. Slice the chicken into thin strips.
9. Warm the pita bread or flatbread in the air fryer for 1-2 minutes.
10. Assemble the shawarma-style chicken by placing the sliced chicken on the warm pita bread.
11. Top with tzatziki sauce or garlic sauce, sliced tomatoes, cucumbers, red onion, and fresh parsley or cilantro.
12. Serve with lemon wedges on the side.

 Prep time: 20 min

 Cook time: 20 min

 Servings: 2

Ingredients

- 2 boneless, skinless chicken breasts (or thighs)
- 2 tbsp olive oil
- 3 cloves garlic, minced
- 1 tbsp fresh lemon juice
- 1 tsp lemon zest
- 1 tsp ground cumin
- 1 tsp ground coriander
- 1 tsp ground paprika
- 1/2 tsp ground turmeric
- 1/2 tsp ground cinnamon
- 1/4 tsp ground allspice
- 1/4 tsp cayenne pepper (optional)
- Salt and pepper to taste
- 1 small red onion, thinly sliced

For Serving:
- Pita bread or flatbread
- Tzatziki sauce or garlic sauce
- Sliced tomatoes
- Sliced cucumbers
- Sliced red onion
- Fresh parsley or cilantro, chopped
- Lemon wedges

Chicken Parmesan

Chicken Parmesan, also known as "chicken parmigiana," is a classic Italian-American dish that has become a beloved comfort food. Traditionally, the chicken is breaded and fried, then topped with marinara sauce and mozzarella cheese before being baked. This air-fried version offers a healthier alternative by using less oil while still achieving a crispy coating and gooey melted cheese. The combination of flavors and textures in Chicken Parmesan makes it a satisfying and delicious meal for any occasion.

Nutrition   Cal 550; Protein 45 g; Fat 25 g; Carb 45 g

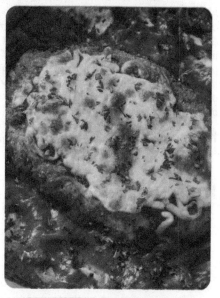

Instructions

1. Preheat your air fryer to 375°F (190°C).
2. Pound the chicken breasts to an even thickness, about 1/2 inch thick, to ensure even cooking.
3. Place the flour in a shallow dish.
4. Place the beaten egg in a second shallow dish.
5. In a third shallow dish, combine the panko breadcrumbs, grated Parmesan cheese, dried oregano, dried basil, garlic powder, onion powder, salt, and pepper.
6. Dredge each chicken breast in the flour, shaking off any excess.
7. Dip the chicken into the beaten egg, ensuring it is well coated.
8. Press the chicken into the breadcrumb mixture, coating it evenly on both sides. Press down to ensure the breadcrumbs adhere well.
9. Lightly spray the air fryer basket with olive oil spray.
10. Place the breaded chicken breasts in the air fryer basket in a single layer. Lightly spray the tops with olive oil spray.
11. Cook for 10-12 minutes, flipping halfway through, until the chicken is golden brown and cooked through.
12. Spoon marinara sauce over each chicken breast.
13. Sprinkle shredded mozzarella cheese evenly over the marinara sauce.
14. Return the chicken to the air fryer and cook for an additional 3-5 minutes until the cheese is melted and bubbly.
15. Garnish with fresh basil or parsley.
16. Serve the chicken Parmesan with a side of pasta, salad, or your favorite vegetable.

 Prep time: 15 min

 Cook time: 20 min

 Servings: 2

Ingredients

- 2 boneless, skinless chicken breasts
- 1/2 cup all-purpose flour
- 1 egg, beaten
- 1 cup panko breadcrumbs
- 1/2 cup grated Parmesan cheese
- 1 tsp dried oregano
- 1 tsp dried basil
- 1/2 tsp garlic powder
- 1/2 tsp onion powder
- Salt and pepper to taste
- Olive oil spray
- 1 cup marinara sauce
- 1 cup shredded mozzarella cheese
- Fresh basil or parsley for garnish

Paprika and Lime Chicken Drumsticks

Paprika, a staple spice in many cuisines, is made from ground dried peppers and adds a rich, smoky flavor to dishes. Combining paprika with lime creates a vibrant and tangy marinade that enhances the natural flavors of the chicken. Air frying the drumsticks results in a crispy exterior while keeping the meat juicy and tender. This dish is not only flavorful but also quick and easy to prepare, making it perfect for a weeknight dinner or a casual gathering.

Nutrition   Cal 400; Protein 35 g; Fat 25 g; Carb 5 g

Instructions

1. In a large bowl, combine the olive oil, minced garlic, paprika, smoked paprika (if using), ground cumin, dried oregano, lime zest, lime juice, salt, and pepper. Mix well.
2. Add the chicken drumsticks to the bowl and toss to coat them evenly with the marinade.
3. Let the chicken marinate for at least 15 minutes, or up to 2 hours for more flavor.
4. Preheat your air fryer to 375°F (190°C).
5. Lightly spray the air fryer basket with olive oil spray.
6. Place the marinated chicken drumsticks in the air fryer basket in a single layer.
7. Cook for 25 minutes, turning halfway through, until the chicken is cooked through and the skin is crispy. The internal temperature should reach 165°F (74°C).
8. Once cooked, remove the chicken drumsticks from the air fryer and let them rest for a few minutes.
9. Garnish with fresh cilantro or parsley.
10. Serve with lime wedges on the side.

 Prep time: 15 min

 Cook time: 25 min

 Servings: 2

Ingredients

- 6 chicken drumsticks
- 2 tbsp olive oil
- 2 cloves garlic, minced
- 1 tbsp paprika
- 1 tsp smoked paprika (optional)
- 1 tsp ground cumin
- 1 tsp dried oregano
- Zest and juice of 1 lime
- Salt and pepper to taste
- Fresh cilantro or parsley for garnish
- Lime wedges for serving

Chicken and Artichoke Hearts

Artichokes have been a staple in Mediterranean cuisine for centuries, valued for their unique flavor and numerous health benefits. They are rich in antioxidants, fiber, and vitamins. When combined with chicken and cooked in an air fryer, the artichokes develop a deliciously crispy texture while maintaining their tender interior. This dish highlights the simplicity and freshness of Mediterranean cooking, making it both a nutritious and flavorful meal option.

Nutrition Cal 400; Protein 35 g; Fat 22 g; Carb 10 g

Instructions

1. In a small bowl, combine the olive oil, minced garlic, dried oregano, dried thyme, lemon zest, lemon juice, salt, and pepper. Mix well.
2. Place the chicken breasts in a resealable plastic bag or a shallow dish.
3. Pour half of the marinade over the chicken, ensuring it is well coated. Seal the bag or cover the dish and let the chicken marinate in the refrigerator for at least 15 minutes.
4. Preheat your air fryer to 375°F (190°C).
5. Remove the chicken breasts from the marinade and place them in the air fryer basket in a single layer.
6. Cook for 15-18 minutes, flipping halfway through, until the chicken is cooked through and reaches an internal temperature of 165°F (74°C).
7. While the chicken is cooking, place the drained and quartered artichoke hearts in a bowl.
8. Toss the artichoke hearts with the remaining marinade and the grated Parmesan cheese.
9. After the chicken has been cooking for 10 minutes, add the artichoke hearts to the air fryer basket around the chicken.
10. Continue cooking for the remaining time until the chicken is done and the artichoke hearts are tender and slightly crispy.
11. Once cooked, remove the chicken and artichoke hearts from the air fryer.
12. Slice the chicken breasts and arrange them on a serving plate with the artichoke hearts.
13. Garnish with fresh parsley and serve immediately.

 Prep time: 15 min

 Cook time: 20 min

 Servings: 2

Ingredients

- 2 boneless, skinless chicken breasts
- 1 can (14 oz) artichoke hearts, drained and quartered
- 2 tbsp olive oil
- 2 cloves garlic, minced
- 1 tsp dried oregano
- 1 tsp dried thyme
- 1 tsp lemon zest
- 1 tbsp fresh lemon juice
- Salt and pepper to taste
- 1/4 cup grated Parmesan cheese
- Fresh parsley for garnish

Moroccan Chicken Drumsticks

Moroccan cuisine is known for its bold and aromatic spices, which create a unique and flavorful profile. The combination of cumin, coriander, paprika, cinnamon, turmeric, and allspice used in this recipe is typical of Moroccan cooking and adds a rich depth of flavor to the chicken. Air frying the drumsticks not only makes the cooking process quicker and healthier but also ensures a crispy exterior while keeping the meat juicy and tender. This dish is a perfect representation of the vibrant and diverse flavors of Moroccan cuisine.

Nutrition Cal 450; Protein 35 g; Fat 28 g; Carb 15 g

Instructions

1. In a large bowl, combine the olive oil, minced garlic, ground cumin, ground coriander, ground paprika, ground cinnamon, ground turmeric, ground allspice, cayenne pepper (if using), lemon juice, lemon zest, salt, and pepper. Mix well.
2. Add the chicken drumsticks to the bowl and toss to coat them evenly with the marinade.
3. Let the chicken marinate for at least 30 minutes, or up to 2 hours for more flavor.
4. Preheat your air fryer to 375°F (190°C).
5. Lightly spray the air fryer basket with olive oil spray.
6. Place the marinated chicken drumsticks in the air fryer basket in a single layer.
7. Cook for 25 minutes, turning halfway through, until the chicken is cooked through and the skin is crispy. The internal temperature should reach 165°F (74°C).
8. Once cooked, remove the chicken drumsticks from the air fryer and let them rest for a few minutes.
9. Garnish with fresh cilantro.
10. Serve with lemon wedges on the side.

 Prep time: 15 min

 Cook time: 25 min

 Servings: 2

Ingredients

- 6 chicken drumsticks
- 2 tbsp olive oil
- 3 cloves garlic, minced
- 1 tsp ground cumin
- 1 tsp ground coriander
- 1 tsp ground paprika
- 1/2 tsp ground cinnamon
- 1/2 tsp ground turmeric
- 1/4 tsp ground allspice
- 1/4 tsp cayenne pepper (optional)
- 1 tbsp fresh lemon juice
- 1 tsp lemon zest
- Salt and pepper to taste
- Fresh cilantro for garnish
- Lemon wedges for serving

Mediterranean Chicken Cordon Bleu

Chicken Cordon Bleu is a classic dish that traditionally features chicken stuffed with ham and cheese, then breaded and fried. This Mediterranean-inspired version uses prosciutto and provolone cheese for a flavorful twist, and air frying ensures a healthier preparation without sacrificing taste or texture. The combination of herbs and Parmesan in the breadcrumb coating adds an extra layer of flavor, making this dish a delicious and elegant meal.

Nutrition   Cal 550; Protein 45 g; Fat 25 g; Carb 30 g

Instructions

1. Preheat your air fryer to 375°F (190°C).
2. Pound the chicken breasts to an even thickness, about 1/4 inch thick, using a meat mallet or rolling pin.
3. Lay 2 slices of prosciutto or turkey ham and 2 slices of cheese on each chicken breast.
4. Roll up the chicken breasts tightly and secure with toothpicks.
5. Place the flour in a shallow dish.
6. Place the beaten egg in a second shallow dish.
7. In a third shallow dish, combine the panko breadcrumbs, grated Parmesan cheese, dried oregano, dried basil, garlic powder, salt, and pepper.
8. Dredge each rolled chicken breast in the flour, shaking off any excess.
9. Dip the chicken into the beaten egg, ensuring it is well coated.
10. Press the chicken into the breadcrumb mixture, coating it evenly on all sides. Press down to ensure the breadcrumbs adhere well.
11. Lightly spray the air fryer basket with olive oil spray.
12. Place the breaded chicken breasts in the air fryer basket in a single layer. Lightly spray the tops with olive oil spray.
13. Cook for 18-20 minutes, flipping halfway through, until the chicken is golden brown and cooked through. The internal temperature should reach 165°F (74°C).
14. Once cooked, remove the chicken from the air fryer and let it rest for a few minutes.
15. Remove the toothpicks before serving.
16. Garnish with fresh parsley and serve with lemon wedges on the side.

 Prep time: 20 min

 Cook time: 20 min

 Servings: 2

Ingredients

- 2 boneless, skinless chicken breasts
- 4 slices prosciutto or turkey ham
- 4 slices provolone or mozzarella cheese
- 1/2 cup all-purpose flour
- 1 egg, beaten
- 1 cup panko breadcrumbs
- 1/2 cup grated Parmesan cheese
- 1 tsp dried oregano
- 1 tsp dried basil
- 1/2 tsp garlic powder
- Salt and pepper to taste
- Olive oil spray
- Fresh parsley for garnish
- Lemon wedges for serving

Crispy Dijon Chicken

Dijon mustard, named after the town of Dijon in Burgundy, France, is known for its sharp and tangy flavor. It pairs beautifully with chicken, adding a layer of complexity to the dish. This recipe combines the tanginess of Dijon mustard with the crunch of panko breadcrumbs and the richness of Parmesan cheese, resulting in a deliciously crispy and flavorful chicken. Air frying ensures a healthier preparation by using less oil, while still achieving a satisfying crunch. This dish is perfect for a quick weeknight dinner or a special meal.

Nutrition Cal 450; Protein 35 g; Fat 20 g; Carb 25 g

Instructions

1. Preheat your air fryer to 375°F (190°C).
2. Pound the chicken breasts to an even thickness, about 1/2 inch thick, using a meat mallet or rolling pin.
3. In a small bowl, combine the Dijon mustard, mayonnaise, and lemon juice. Mix well.
4. 3.Prepare the Breading:
5. In a shallow dish, combine the panko breadcrumbs, grated Parmesan cheese, dried thyme, dried rosemary, garlic powder, salt, and pepper.
6. Brush each chicken breast with the Dijon mustard mixture, ensuring they are well coated.
7. Press the chicken into the breadcrumb mixture, coating it evenly on all sides. Press down to ensure the breadcrumbs adhere well.
8. Lightly spray the air fryer basket with olive oil spray.
9. Place the breaded chicken breasts in the air fryer basket in a single layer. Lightly spray the tops with olive oil spray.
10. Cook for 18-20 minutes, flipping halfway through, until the chicken is golden brown and cooked through. The internal temperature should reach 165°F (74°C).
11. Once cooked, remove the chicken from the air fryer and let it rest for a few minutes.
12. Garnish with fresh parsley and serve with lemon wedges on the side.

 Prep time: 15 min

 Cook time: 20 min

 Servings: 2

Ingredients

- 2 boneless, skinless chicken breasts
- 2 tbsp Dijon mustard
- 2 tbsp mayonnaise
- 1 tsp lemon juice
- 1/2 cup panko breadcrumbs
- 1/4 cup grated Parmesan cheese
- 1 tsp dried thyme
- 1 tsp dried rosemary
- 1/2 tsp garlic powder
- Salt and pepper to taste
- Olive oil spray
- Fresh parsley for garnish
- Lemon wedges for serving

Chicken and Olive Tagine

Tagine is a traditional North African dish named after the earthenware pot in which it is cooked. The unique shape of the tagine pot helps to steam the food while it simmers, creating tender, flavorful dishes. While this recipe is adapted for an air fryer, it retains the classic combination of spices and ingredients that give tagine its distinctive flavor. The preserved lemons and olives add a tangy and salty complexity, complementing the rich spices and tender chicken. This dish showcases the vibrant and aromatic qualities of Moroccan cuisine.

Nutrition   Cal 500; Protein 35 g; Fat 35 g; Carb 10 g

Instructions

1. Preheat your air fryer to 375°F (190°C).
2. Season the chicken thighs with salt and pepper.
3. Place the chicken thighs in the air fryer basket, skin side up, and cook for 10 minutes until the skin is crispy and browned. Remove from the air fryer and set aside.
4. In a large skillet, heat the olive oil over medium heat.
5. Add the finely chopped onion and sauté until softened, about 3-5 minutes.
6. Add the minced garlic, ground cumin, ground coriander, ground turmeric, ground ginger, ground cinnamon, and cayenne pepper (if using). Cook for another 1-2 minutes until fragrant.
7. Stir in the green olives, chicken broth, and preserved lemons.
8. Return the browned chicken thighs to the skillet, nestling them into the mixture. Spoon some of the sauce over the chicken.
9. Carefully transfer the mixture from the skillet to an air fryer-safe dish that fits in your air fryer basket.
10. Place the dish in the air fryer and cook for an additional 20 minutes, or until the chicken is cooked through and tender. The internal temperature should reach 165°F (74°C).
11. Garnish with chopped fresh parsley before serving.
12. Serve hot with couscous, rice, or flatbread.

 Prep time: 20 min

 Cook time: 30 min

 Servings: 2

Ingredients

- 4 bone-in, skin-on chicken thighs
- 2 tbsp olive oil
- 1 onion, finely chopped
- 3 cloves garlic, minced
- 1 tsp ground cumin
- 1 tsp ground coriander
- 1 tsp ground turmeric
- 1 tsp ground ginger
- 1/2 tsp ground cinnamon
- 1/4 tsp cayenne pepper (optional)
- 1/2 cup green olives, pitted and halved
- 1/2 cup chicken broth
- 1/4 cup preserved lemons, chopped
- 1/4 cup chopped fresh parsley
- Salt and pepper to taste

Chicken Caprese

The Caprese salad, from which this dish is inspired, originates from the Italian island of Capri. It traditionally consists of fresh tomatoes, mozzarella, and basil, representing the colors of the Italian flag. This Chicken Caprese recipe takes those classic flavors and combines them with juicy, seasoned chicken breasts, creating a delicious and balanced meal. Air frying ensures the chicken is perfectly cooked with a crispy exterior, while the fresh mozzarella and cherry tomatoes add a creamy and tangy contrast. The balsamic glaze finishes the dish with a sweet and tangy note, making it a delightful dinner option.

Nutrition Cal 450; Protein 40 g; Fat 25 g; Carb 10 g

Instructions

1. Preheat your air fryer to 375°F (190°C).
2. Pound the chicken breasts to an even thickness, about 1/2 inch thick, using a meat mallet or rolling pin.
3. In a small bowl, combine the olive oil, minced garlic, salt, pepper, dried oregano, and dried basil. Mix well.
4. Brush the mixture evenly over both sides of the chicken breasts.
5. Place the seasoned chicken breasts in the air fryer basket in a single layer.
6. Cook for 15 minutes, flipping halfway through, until the chicken is cooked through and reaches an internal temperature of 165°F (74°C).
7. While the chicken is cooking, place the halved cherry tomatoes in a bowl and toss them with a little olive oil, salt, and pepper.
8. After 15 minutes of cooking, open the air fryer and top each chicken breast with two slices of fresh mozzarella cheese and a handful of the seasoned cherry tomatoes.
9. Cook for an additional 5 minutes, or until the cheese is melted and bubbly.
10. Once cooked, remove the chicken breasts from the air fryer and let them rest for a few minutes.
11. Garnish with fresh basil leaves.
12. Drizzle with balsamic glaze before serving.

 Prep time: 15 min

 Cook time: 20 min

 Servings: 2

Ingredients

- 2 boneless, skinless chicken breasts
- 2 tbsp olive oil
- 2 cloves garlic, minced
- Salt and pepper to taste
- 1 tsp dried oregano
- 1 tsp dried basil
- 1 cup cherry tomatoes, halved
- 4 slices fresh mozzarella cheese
- Fresh basil leaves for garnish
- Balsamic glaze for drizzling

Greek Turkey Meatballs

Greek cuisine is known for its use of fresh herbs, spices, and simple ingredients that create vibrant and flavorful dishes. These Greek Turkey Meatballs are no exception, featuring a blend of herbs like parsley and mint, along with feta cheese and classic Mediterranean spices. Air frying the meatballs ensures they are cooked to perfection with a crispy exterior and juicy interior, while using less oil than traditional frying methods. This dish is a great option for a healthy and delicious meal that captures the essence of Greek flavors.

Nutrition Cal 300; Protein 25 g; Fat 15 g; Carb 15 g

Instructions

1. In a large bowl, combine the ground turkey, finely chopped red onion, minced garlic, chopped parsley, chopped mint, crumbled feta cheese, breadcrumbs, lightly beaten egg, dried oregano, ground cumin, ground coriander, salt, and pepper. Mix well until all ingredients are evenly incorporated.
2. Divide the mixture into equal portions and shape each portion into meatballs, about 1 inch in diameter. This recipe should make about 16-20 meatballs, depending on size.
3. Preheat your air fryer to 375°F (190°C).
4. Lightly spray the air fryer basket with olive oil spray.
5. Place the meatballs in the air fryer basket in a single layer, ensuring they do not touch.
6. Cook for 12-15 minutes, shaking the basket halfway through, until the meatballs are browned and cooked through.
7. Serve the meatballs with tzatziki sauce, pita bread or flatbread, sliced cucumbers, sliced tomatoes, red onion slices, and garnish with fresh parsley or mint.

 Prep time: 20 min

 Cook time: 15 min

 Servings: 4

Ingredients

- 1 lb ground turkey
- 1/4 cup red onion, finely chopped
- 2 cloves garlic, minced
- 1/4 cup fresh parsley, chopped
- 1/4 cup fresh mint, chopped
- 1/4 cup crumbled feta cheese
- 1/4 cup breadcrumbs (or almond flour for a gluten-free option)
- 1 egg, lightly beaten
- 1 tsp dried oregano
- 1/2 tsp ground cumin
- 1/2 tsp ground coriander
- Salt and pepper to taste
- Olive oil spray

Lemon Garlic Rosemary Turkey Breasts

Turkey is a lean and nutritious protein option, often enjoyed during festive meals but also perfect for everyday dinners. This recipe infuses the turkey breasts with the bright flavors of lemon and the aromatic notes of garlic and rosemary. Air frying ensures that the turkey remains juicy and tender while developing a deliciously crispy exterior. The combination of these Mediterranean-inspired ingredients not only enhances the taste but also offers a healthy and satisfying meal.

Nutrition   Cal 350; Protein 20 g; Fat 20 g; Carb 5 g

Instructions

1. In a small bowl, combine the olive oil, minced garlic, chopped rosemary, lemon juice, lemon zest, salt, and pepper. Mix well.
2. Place the turkey breasts in a resealable plastic bag or a shallow dish.
3. Pour the marinade over the turkey breasts, ensuring they are well coated.
4. Seal the bag or cover the dish and let the turkey marinate in the refrigerator for at least 30 minutes, or up to 2 hours for more flavor.
5. Preheat your air fryer to 375°F (190°C).
6. Remove the turkey breasts from the marinade and place them in the air fryer basket in a single layer.
7. Cook for 20-25 minutes, flipping halfway through, until the turkey is cooked through and reaches an internal temperature of 165°F (74°C).
8. Once cooked, remove the turkey breasts from the air fryer and let them rest for 5 minutes to allow the juices to redistribute.
9. Slice the turkey breasts and arrange them on a serving plate.
10. Garnish with fresh parsley and serve with lemon wedges on the side.

 Prep time: 15 min

 Cook time: 25 min

 Servings: 2

Ingredients

- 2 boneless, skinless turkey breasts
- 2 tbsp olive oil
- 3 cloves garlic, minced
- 1 tbsp fresh rosemary, chopped (or 1 tsp dried rosemary)
- 1 tbsp fresh lemon juice
- 1 tsp lemon zest
- Salt and pepper to taste
- Fresh parsley for garnish
- Lemon wedges for serving

Spiced Turkey Patties with Pepper Sauce

Turkey is a versatile and lean protein that can be spiced and flavored in various ways. This recipe incorporates a blend of Middle Eastern spices, giving the turkey patties a warm and aromatic flavor profile. The accompanying roasted red pepper sauce adds a sweet and tangy contrast, enhancing the overall taste experience. Air frying the patties ensures they are cooked evenly and remain juicy inside while developing a crispy exterior. This dish is a great example of how to combine different culinary traditions to create a healthy and delicious meal.

Nutrition   Cal 450; Protein 35 g; Fat 25 g; Carb 20 g

Instructions

1. In a large bowl, combine the ground turkey, finely chopped red onion, minced garlic, chopped parsley, ground cumin, smoked paprika, ground coriander, ground cinnamon, cayenne pepper (if using), salt, pepper, lightly beaten egg, and breadcrumbs. Mix well until all ingredients are evenly incorporated.
2. Divide the mixture into equal portions and shape each portion into patties, about 1 inch thick. This recipe should make about 4-6 patties, depending on size.
3. Preheat your air fryer to 375°F (190°C).
4. Lightly spray the air fryer basket with olive oil spray.
5. Place the patties in the air fryer basket in a single layer, ensuring they do not touch.
6. Cook for 12-15 minutes, flipping halfway through, until the patties are browned and cooked through. The internal temperature should reach 165°F (74°C).
7. In a blender or food processor, combine the roasted red bell pepper, minced garlic, Greek yogurt, olive oil, lemon juice, salt, and pepper. Blend until smooth.
8. Once the patties are cooked, remove them from the air fryer and let them rest for a few minutes.
9. Serve the turkey patties with the pepper sauce on the side.

 Prep time: 20 min

 Cook time: 15 min

 Servings: 2

Ingredients

For the Turkey Patties:
- 1 lb ground turkey
- 1/4 cup red onion, finely chopped
- 2 cloves garlic, minced
- 1/4 cup fresh parsley, chopped
- 1 tsp ground cumin
- 1 tsp smoked paprika
- 1/2 tsp ground coriander
- 1/2 tsp ground cinnamon
- 1/4 tsp cayenne pepper (optional)
- Salt and pepper to taste
- 1 egg, lightly beaten
- 1/4 cup breadcrumbs (or almond flour for a gluten-free option)
- Olive oil spray

For the Pepper Sauce:
- 1 red bell pepper, roasted and peeled
- 1 clove garlic, minced
- 1/4 cup Greek yogurt
- 1 tbsp olive oil
- 1 tsp lemon juice
- Salt and pepper to taste

Turkey and Spinach Pinwheels

Pinwheels are a popular party appetizer that can be filled with a variety of ingredients. This version combines the lean protein of turkey with the nutritious benefits of spinach and the creamy texture of cheese, all wrapped in a flaky puff pastry. Air frying the pinwheels ensures they are crispy on the outside while the filling remains tender and flavorful. These Turkey and Spinach Pinwheels are not only delicious but also visually appealing, making them a great addition to any gathering or as a fun snack.

Nutrition Cal 400; Protein 20 g; Fat 25 g; Carb 30 g

Instructions

1. Preheat your air fryer to 375°F (190°C).
2. On a lightly floured surface, roll out the puff pastry sheet into a rectangle, about 1/4 inch thick.
3. Spread the softened cream cheese evenly over the puff pastry sheet.
4. Layer the thinly sliced turkey breast evenly on top of the cream cheese.
5. Spread the fresh spinach leaves over the turkey.
6. Sprinkle the grated Parmesan cheese and chopped sun-dried tomatoes over the spinach.
7. Season with salt and pepper to taste.
8. Starting from one of the longer sides, tightly roll up the puff pastry into a log.
9. Slice the log into 1/2 inch thick pinwheels.
10. Lightly spray the air fryer basket with olive oil spray.
11. Place the pinwheels in the air fryer basket in a single layer, leaving a little space between each pinwheel.
12. Brush the tops of the pinwheels with the beaten egg for a golden finish.
13. Air fry the pinwheels for 8-10 minutes, or until the pastry is golden brown and crispy.
14. Once cooked, remove the pinwheels from the air fryer and let them cool for a few minutes before serving.
15. Serve warm, as an appetizer or a snack.

 Prep time: 20 min

 Cook time: 10 min

 Servings: 2

Ingredients

- 1 package puff pastry (thawed, if frozen)
- 1/2 lb thinly sliced turkey breast (deli style)
- 1 cup fresh spinach leaves
- 1/2 cup cream cheese, softened
- 1/4 cup grated Parmesan cheese
- 1/4 cup sun-dried tomatoes, chopped
- 1 egg, lightly beaten (for egg wash)
- Salt and pepper to taste

Turkey and Vegetable Skewers with Tomato Sauce

Skewers, also known as kebabs, are a popular method of cooking meat and vegetables in many cultures. This recipe combines the lean protein of turkey with a variety of colorful vegetables, making it a healthy and visually appealing dish. Air frying ensures the skewers are cooked evenly and quickly, with minimal oil. The homemade tomato sauce adds a fresh and tangy flavor, complementing the grilled taste of the skewers. This dish is perfect for a quick weeknight dinner or a fun and healthy meal option for gatherings.

Nutrition Cal 450; Protein 35 g; Fat 20 g; Carb 25 g

Instructions

1. In a large bowl, combine the olive oil, minced garlic, dried oregano, dried thyme, salt, and pepper. Mix well.
2. Add the turkey cubes, zucchini slices, red bell pepper pieces, red onion pieces, and cherry tomatoes to the bowl. Toss to coat evenly with the marinade.
3. Thread the turkey and vegetables onto the skewers, alternating between turkey and vegetables.
4. Preheat your air fryer to 375°F (190°C).
5. Place the skewers in the air fryer basket in a single layer.
6. Cook for 12-15 minutes, turning halfway through, until the turkey is cooked through and the vegetables are tender and slightly charred. The internal temperature of the turkey should reach 165°F (74°C).
7. While the skewers are cooking, heat the olive oil in a saucepan over medium heat.
8. Add the finely chopped red onion and minced garlic, and sauté until softened, about 3-4 minutes.
9. Add the diced tomatoes, dried basil, dried oregano, salt, and pepper. Simmer for 10-15 minutes, stirring occasionally, until the sauce thickens.
10. Once the skewers are cooked, remove them from the air fryer.
11. Serve the skewers with the tomato sauce on the side for dipping or drizzling.

 Prep time: 20 min

 Cook time: 15 min

 Servings: 2

Ingredients

- 1 lb turkey breast, cut into 1-inch cubes
- 1 zucchini, sliced into rounds
- 1 red bell pepper, cut into 1-inch pieces
- 1 red onion, cut into 1-inch pieces
- 8-10 cherry tomatoes
- 2 tbsp olive oil
- 2 cloves garlic, minced
- 1 tsp dried oregano
- 1 tsp dried thyme
- Salt and pepper to taste
- Wooden or metal skewers (if using wooden, soak in water for 30 minutes)

For the Tomato Sauce:
- 1 can (14.5 oz) diced tomatoes
- 2 cloves garlic, minced
- 1/4 cup red onion, finely chopped
- 1 tbsp olive oil
- 1 tsp dried basil
- 1 tsp dried oregano
- Salt and pepper to taste

Garlic and Herb Turkey Tenderloin

Turkey tenderloin is a lean and tender cut of meat that absorbs flavors well, making it perfect for marinades. The combination of garlic, herbs, and lemon in this recipe infuses the turkey with vibrant and aromatic flavors, while air frying ensures the meat remains juicy and tender with a slightly crispy exterior. This dish is a healthy and delicious option that showcases the simplicity and freshness of Mediterranean-inspired cooking.

Nutrition
Cal 350; Protein 30 g; Fat 20 g; Carb 5 g

Instructions

1. In a small bowl, combine the olive oil, minced garlic, chopped rosemary, chopped thyme, chopped parsley, lemon zest, lemon juice, salt, and pepper. Mix well.
2. Place the turkey tenderloin in a resealable plastic bag or a shallow dish.
3. Pour the marinade over the turkey, ensuring it is well coated.
4. Seal the bag or cover the dish and let the turkey marinate in the refrigerator for at least 30 minutes, or up to 2 hours for more flavor.
5. Preheat your air fryer to 375°F (190°C).
6. Remove the turkey tenderloin from the marinade and place it in the air fryer basket.
7. Cook for 20-25 minutes, flipping halfway through, until the turkey is cooked through and reaches an internal temperature of 165°F (74°C).
8. Once cooked, remove the turkey tenderloin from the air fryer and let it rest for 5 minutes to allow the juices to redistribute.
9. Slice the turkey tenderloin and arrange it on a serving plate.
10. Garnish with fresh parsley and serve with lemon wedges on the side.

 Prep time: 15 min

 Cook time: 25 min

 Servings: 2

Ingredients

- 1 lb turkey tenderloin
- 2 tbsp olive oil
- 3 cloves garlic, minced
- 1 tbsp fresh rosemary, chopped (or 1 tsp dried rosemary)
- 1 tbsp fresh thyme, chopped (or 1 tsp dried thyme)
- 1 tbsp fresh parsley, chopped
- 1 tsp lemon zest
- 1 tbsp fresh lemon juice
- Salt and pepper to taste
- Fresh parsley for garnish
- Lemon wedges for serving

Turkey Croquettes with Dip

Croquettes are a versatile dish that can be made with a variety of ingredients and are popular in many cultures. This recipe uses leftover turkey and mashed potatoes, making it a great way to utilize leftovers from holiday meals. The combination of crispy exterior and flavorful, moist interior makes these croquettes a delicious and satisfying appetizer or snack. The accompanying dip adds a refreshing tanginess that complements the savory croquettes perfectly. Air frying ensures a healthier preparation by using less oil while still achieving a crunchy texture.

Nutrition   Cal 400; Protein 25 g; Fat 20 g; Carb 30 g

Instructions

1. In a large bowl, combine the finely chopped turkey, mashed potatoes, finely chopped onion, minced garlic, chopped parsley, dried thyme, paprika, salt, and pepper. Mix well until all ingredients are evenly incorporated.
2. Take about 2 tablespoons of the mixture and shape it into a small log or ball. Repeat with the remaining mixture.
3. Place the beaten egg in a shallow dish.
4. In another shallow dish, combine the panko breadcrumbs and grated Parmesan cheese.
5. Dip each croquette in the beaten egg, then roll it in the breadcrumb mixture, pressing gently to adhere. Place the breaded croquettes on a plate.
6. Preheat your air fryer to 375°F (190°C).
7. Lightly spray the air fryer basket with olive oil spray.
8. Place the croquettes in the air fryer basket in a single layer, ensuring they do not touch.
9. Lightly spray the tops of the croquettes with olive oil spray.
10. Cook for 10-15 minutes, turning halfway through, until the croquettes are golden brown and crispy.
11. In a small bowl, combine the Greek yogurt, mayonnaise, lemon juice, minced garlic, chopped dill, salt, and pepper. Mix well.
12. Once the croquettes are cooked, remove them from the air fryer and let them cool slightly.
13. Serve the turkey croquettes with the prepared dip on the side.

 Prep time: 25 min

 Cook time: 15 min

 Servings: 2

Ingredients

- 2 cups cooked turkey, finely chopped
- 1/2 cup mashed potatoes
- 1/4 cup finely chopped onion
- 2 cloves garlic, minced
- 1/4 cup fresh parsley, chopped
- 1 tsp dried thyme
- 1 tsp paprika
- Salt and pepper to taste
- 1 egg, lightly beaten
- 1 cup panko breadcrumbs
- 1/2 cup grated Parmesan cheese
- Olive oil spray

For the Dip:
- 1/2 cup Greek yogurt
- 1/4 cup mayonnaise
- 1 tbsp lemon juice
- 1 clove garlic, minced
- 1 tbsp fresh dill, chopped
- Salt and pepper to taste

Turkey Zucchini Lasagna

Lasagna is a beloved dish in many cultures, traditionally made with pasta. This zucchini version is a healthier alternative that reduces carbs and adds extra vegetables to your meal. The use of ground turkey instead of beef further lightens the dish, making it a nutritious yet satisfying option. Air frying the lasagna ensures it is cooked evenly and quickly, resulting in a deliciously cheesy and hearty meal with a perfectly tender texture.

Nutrition   Cal 350; Protein 30 g; Fat 20 g; Carb 10 g

Instructions

1. In a large skillet, heat the olive oil over medium heat.
2. Add the finely chopped onion and minced garlic, and sauté until fragrant and softened, about 3-4 minutes.
3. Add the ground turkey to the skillet and cook until browned, breaking it up with a spoon, about 5-7 minutes.
4. Stir in the diced tomatoes, tomato paste, dried oregano, dried basil, salt, and pepper. Simmer for 10-15 minutes, until the sauce thickens.
5. Slice the zucchinis lengthwise into thin strips using a mandoline or a sharp knife.
6. Lightly salt the zucchini slices and let them sit for 10 minutes to draw out excess moisture. Pat them dry with a paper towel.
7. In a medium bowl, combine the ricotta cheese, lightly beaten egg, and grated Parmesan cheese. Mix well.
8. Preheat your air fryer to 375°F (190°C).
9. In an air fryer-safe dish, spread a thin layer of the turkey sauce on the bottom.
10. Layer with zucchini slices, followed by a layer of the ricotta mixture, then a layer of turkey sauce.
11. Repeat the layers until all ingredients are used, finishing with a layer of turkey sauce.
12. Sprinkle the shredded mozzarella cheese on top.
13. Place the assembled lasagna in the air fryer basket.
14. Cook for 20-25 minutes, until the cheese is melted and bubbly and the zucchini is tender.
15. If the top browns too quickly, cover it with aluminum foil and continue cooking.
16. Once cooked, remove the lasagna from the air fryer and let it rest for a few minutes before slicing.
17. Garnish with fresh basil or parsley before serving.

 Prep time: 25 min

 Cook time: 25 min

 Servings: 4

Ingredients

For the Turkey Sauce:
- 1 lb ground turkey
- 1/2 cup onion, finely chopped
- 2 cloves garlic, minced
- 1 can (14.5 oz) diced tomatoes
- 1/4 cup tomato paste
- 1 tsp dried oregano
- 1 tsp dried basil
- Salt and pepper to taste
- 1 tbsp olive oil

For the Lasagna:
- 2 large zucchinis, sliced lengthwise into thin strips
- 1 cup ricotta cheese
- 1 egg, lightly beaten
- 1/4 cup grated Parmesan cheese
- 1 cup shredded mozzarella cheese
- Fresh basil or parsley for garnish

Mediterranean Turkey Salad

The Mediterranean diet is celebrated for its health benefits, particularly for heart health and longevity. This turkey salad is a perfect example of Mediterranean cuisine, featuring lean protein, fresh vegetables, and healthy fats. The combination of marinated and air-fried turkey with crisp greens, tangy feta, and a zesty homemade dressing creates a delicious and nutritious meal. This salad is not only refreshing and flavorful but also packed with nutrients, making it an excellent choice for a healthy lunch or dinner.

Nutrition Cal 450; Protein 35 g; Fat 30 g; Carb 15 g

Instructions

1. In a large skillet, heat the olive oil over medium heat.
2. Add the finely chopped onion and minced garlic, and sauté until fragrant and softened, about 3-4 minutes.
3. Add the ground turkey to the skillet and cook until browned, breaking it up with a spoon, about 5-7 minutes.
4. Stir in the diced tomatoes, tomato paste, dried oregano, dried basil, salt, and pepper. Simmer for 10-15 minutes, until the sauce thickens.
5. Slice the zucchinis lengthwise into thin strips using a mandoline or a sharp knife.
6. Lightly salt the zucchini slices and let them sit for 10 minutes to draw out excess moisture. Pat them dry with a paper towel.
7. In a medium bowl, combine the ricotta cheese, lightly beaten egg, and grated Parmesan cheese. Mix well.
8. Preheat your air fryer to 375°F (190°C).
9. In an air fryer-safe dish, spread a thin layer of the turkey sauce on the bottom.
10. Layer with zucchini slices, followed by a layer of the ricotta mixture, then a layer of turkey sauce.
11. Repeat the layers until all ingredients are used, finishing with a layer of turkey sauce.
12. Sprinkle the shredded mozzarella cheese on top.
13. Place the assembled lasagna in the air fryer basket.
14. Cook for 20-25 minutes, until the cheese is melted and bubbly and the zucchini is tender.
15. If the top browns too quickly, cover it with aluminum foil and continue cooking.
16. Once cooked, remove the lasagna from the air fryer and let it rest for a few minutes before slicing.
17. Garnish with fresh basil or parsley before serving.

 Prep time: 20 min

 Cook time: 10 min

 Servings: 2

Ingredients

For the Turkey:
- 1 lb turkey breast, cut into strips
- 2 tbsp olive oil
- 2 cloves garlic, minced
- 1 tsp dried oregano
- 1 tsp dried thyme
- 1 tsp smoked paprika
- Salt and pepper to taste

For the Salad:
- 4 cups mixed greens (such as romaine, arugula, and spinach)
- 1 cup cherry tomatoes, halved
- 1 cucumber, diced
- 1/4 red onion, thinly sliced
- 1/4 cup Kalamata olives, pitted and halved
- 1/4 cup feta cheese, crumbled
- 1/4 cup roasted red peppers, sliced

For the Dressing:
- 1/4 cup olive oil
- 2 tbsp red wine vinegar
- 1 tbsp fresh lemon juice
- 1 tsp Dijon mustard
- 1 clove garlic, minced
- 1 tsp dried oregano

Ground Turkey with Vegetables

Ground turkey is a versatile and lean protein that can be paired with a variety of vegetables to create a nutritious and balanced meal. This dish highlights the fresh and vibrant flavors of Mediterranean cuisine, combining a mix of colorful vegetables with savory ground turkey. Air frying the vegetables ensures they retain their nutrients and develop a deliciously charred flavor, while the ground turkey adds a hearty element to the dish. This recipe is quick, healthy, and perfect for a weeknight dinner.

Nutrition   Cal 400; Protein 35 g; Fat 22 g; Carb 15 g

Instructions

1. In a large bowl, combine the chopped red bell pepper, zucchini, yellow squash, cherry tomatoes, red onion, and minced garlic.
2. Drizzle with olive oil and sprinkle with dried oregano, dried basil, smoked paprika, salt, and pepper. Toss to coat evenly.
3. Preheat your air fryer to 375°F (190°C).
4. Place the seasoned vegetables in the air fryer basket in a single layer.
5. Cook for 10 minutes, shaking the basket halfway through, until the vegetables are tender and slightly charred.
6. While the vegetables are cooking, heat a skillet over medium-high heat.
7. Add the ground turkey to the skillet and cook, breaking it up with a spoon, until browned and cooked through, about 7-8 minutes.
8. Season with salt and pepper to taste.
9. Once the vegetables are cooked, add them to the skillet with the cooked ground turkey. Stir to combine and heat through for an additional 2-3 minutes.
10. Garnish with fresh parsley before serving.

 Prep time: 15 min

 Cook time: 15 min

 Servings: 2

Ingredients

- 1 lb ground turkey
- 1 red bell pepper, chopped
- 1 zucchini, chopped
- 1 yellow squash, chopped
- 1 cup cherry tomatoes, halved
- 1/2 cup red onion, finely chopped
- 2 cloves garlic, minced
- 2 tbsp olive oil
- 1 tsp dried oregano
- 1 tsp dried basil
- 1/2 tsp smoked paprika
- Salt and pepper to taste

Fresh parsley for garnish

FISH AND SEAFOOD

Lemon and Herb Sardines

Sardines are a nutrient-dense food, rich in omega-3 fatty acids, protein, vitamins, and minerals. They are a staple in Mediterranean cuisine, known for their health benefits, including promoting heart health and reducing inflammation. Air frying sardines enhances their natural flavor while creating a crispy texture, making them a delicious and healthy option. This recipe combines the bright flavors of lemon and fresh herbs, adding a refreshing and aromatic touch to the sardines. Serving them with lemon wedges adds an extra burst of citrus flavor, making this dish a perfect appetizer or light meal.

Nutrition   Cal 300; Protein 25 g; Fat 20 g; Carb 2 g

Instructions

1. In a small bowl, combine the olive oil, minced garlic, lemon juice, lemon zest, chopped parsley, chopped dill, dried oregano, salt, and pepper. Mix well.
2. Place the cleaned sardines in a shallow dish or a resealable plastic bag.
3. Pour the marinade over the sardines, ensuring they are well coated.
4. Let the sardines marinate for at least 15 minutes.
5. Preheat your air fryer to 400°F (200°C).
6. Lightly spray the air fryer basket with olive oil spray.
7. Place the marinated sardines in the air fryer basket in a single layer.
8. Cook for 8-10 minutes, turning halfway through, until the sardines are crispy and golden brown.
9. Once cooked, remove the sardines from the air fryer and let them cool for a few minutes.
10. Serve with lemon wedges on the side.

 Prep time: 15 min

 Cook time: 10 min

 Servings: 2

Ingredients

- 8 fresh sardines, cleaned and gutted
- 3 tbsp olive oil
- 2 cloves garlic, minced
- 1 tbsp fresh lemon juice
- 1 tsp lemon zest
- 1 tbsp fresh parsley, chopped
- 1 tbsp fresh dill, chopped
- 1 tsp dried oregano
- Salt and pepper to taste
- Lemon wedges for serving

Anchovy and Tomato Crostini

Crostini, meaning "little toasts" in Italian, are a popular appetizer or snack in Mediterranean cuisine. The combination of anchovies and tomatoes brings together the umami-rich, salty flavor of anchovies with the sweet and juicy taste of tomatoes. Air frying the baguette slices ensures they are perfectly crispy with minimal oil, making this dish a healthier option. The fresh herbs add a burst of color and flavor, while the optional balsamic glaze provides a tangy sweetness that complements the savory topping. This simple yet delicious crostini is perfect for entertaining or as a light appetizer.

Nutrition   Cal 250; Protein 8 g; Fat 12 g; Carb 28 g

Instructions

1. Preheat your air fryer to 375°F (190°C).
2. Brush both sides of the baguette slices with olive oil.
3. Place the baguette slices in the air fryer basket in a single layer.
4. Toast for 3-5 minutes until golden brown and crispy.
5. Once toasted, rub the cut sides of the garlic clove over the top of each baguette slice for added flavor.
6. In a small bowl, combine the halved cherry tomatoes, chopped anchovy fillets, chopped basil, and chopped parsley.
7. Season with salt and pepper to taste. Be mindful with the salt since anchovies are naturally salty.
8. Spoon the tomato and anchovy mixture onto each toasted baguette slice.
9. Arrange the crostini on a serving plate.
10. Drizzle with balsamic glaze if desired.
11. Serve immediately while the crostini are still warm.

 Prep time: 10 min

 Cook time: 5 min

 Servings: 2

Ingredients

- 1 baguette, sliced into 1/2 inch rounds
- 2 tbsp olive oil
- 1 garlic clove, halved
- 8 cherry tomatoes, halved
- 4 anchovy fillets, drained and chopped
- 1 tbsp fresh basil, chopped
- 1 tbsp fresh parsley, chopped
- Salt and pepper to taste
- Balsamic glaze for drizzling (optional)

Tuna Steaks with Capers

Tuna steaks are a great source of lean protein and omega-3 fatty acids, which are beneficial for heart health. Cooking tuna steaks in an air fryer helps to retain their natural moisture while creating a perfectly seared exterior. The addition of capers, which are pickled flower buds, brings a burst of tangy and briny flavor that complements the rich taste of the tuna. This dish is quick to prepare and cook, making it a perfect option for a healthy and delicious weeknight dinner.

Nutrition Cal 350; Protein 35 g; Fat 22 g; Carb 2 g

Instructions

1. In a small bowl, combine the olive oil, minced garlic, lemon juice, lemon zest, salt, and pepper. Mix well.
2. Place the tuna steaks in a shallow dish or resealable plastic bag.
3. Pour the marinade over the tuna steaks, ensuring they are well coated.
4. Let the tuna marinate in the refrigerator for at least 15 minutes.
5. Preheat your air fryer to 400°F (200°C).
6. Remove the tuna steaks from the marinade and place them in the air fryer basket in a single layer.
7. Cook for 4-5 minutes per side for medium-rare, or until the desired doneness is reached. Be careful not to overcook, as tuna can become dry.
8. While the tuna is cooking, lightly sauté the capers in a small pan over medium heat for 1-2 minutes until they are slightly crispy.
9. Once the tuna steaks are cooked, remove them from the air fryer and let them rest for a few minutes.
10. Garnish with crispy capers and fresh parsley.
11. Serve with lemon wedges on the side.

 Prep time: 15 min

 Cook time: 10 min

Servings: 2

Ingredients

- 2 tuna steaks (about 6 oz each)
- 2 tbsp olive oil
- 2 cloves garlic, minced
- 1 tbsp lemon juice
- 1 tsp lemon zest
- 1 tbsp capers, drained
- Salt and pepper to taste
- Fresh parsley for garnish
- Lemon wedges for serving

Halibut with Garlic Lemon Aioli

Halibut is a lean, white fish that is rich in protein and essential nutrients such as selenium, magnesium, and vitamins B6 and B12. Cooking halibut in an air fryer helps retain its moisture and results in a perfectly flaky texture. The garlic lemon aioli adds a creamy and tangy flavor that complements the mild taste of the halibut, making this dish both delicious and nutritious. This recipe is a great option for a quick and healthy dinner that can be enjoyed any night of the week.

Nutrition   Cal 450; Protein 35 g; Fat 30 g; Carb 3 g

Instructions

1. In a small bowl, combine the olive oil, minced garlic, lemon juice, lemon zest, salt, and pepper. Mix well.
2. Place the halibut fillets in a shallow dish or resealable plastic bag.
3. Pour the marinade over the halibut, ensuring the fillets are well coated.
4. Let the halibut marinate in the refrigerator for at least 15 minutes.
5. Preheat your air fryer to 375°F (190°C).
6. Remove the halibut fillets from the marinade and place them in the air fryer basket in a single layer.
7. Cook for 12-15 minutes, depending on the thickness of the fillets, until the halibut is cooked through and flakes easily with a fork.
8. In a small bowl, combine the mayonnaise, minced garlic, lemon juice, lemon zest, chopped parsley, salt, and pepper. Mix well until smooth.
9. Once the halibut is cooked, remove it from the air fryer and let it rest for a few minutes.
10. Serve the halibut fillets with a dollop of garlic lemon aioli on top.
11. Garnish with fresh parsley and serve with lemon wedges on the side.

 Prep time: 15 min

 Cook time: 15 min

 Servings: 2

Ingredients

- 2 halibut fillets (about 6 oz each)
- 2 tbsp olive oil
- 2 cloves garlic, minced
- 1 tbsp lemon juice
- 1 tsp lemon zest
- Salt and pepper to taste
- Fresh parsley for garnish
- Lemon wedges for serving

For the Garlic Lemon Aioli:
- 1/2 cup mayonnaise
- 2 cloves garlic, minced
- 1 tbsp lemon juice
- 1 tsp lemon zest
- 1 tbsp fresh parsley, chopped
- Salt and pepper to taste

Tilapia with Olive Tapenade

Tilapia is a mild-flavored, white fish that is popular for its versatility and quick cooking time. It is a good source of protein and low in fat. The olive tapenade, a classic Mediterranean condiment made from olives, capers, and garlic, adds a burst of flavor to the tilapia, enhancing its taste with a savory and tangy profile. Air frying the tilapia ensures a moist and flaky texture while using minimal oil, making this dish a healthy and delicious option for a quick and easy dinner.

Nutrition   Cal 350; Protein 30 g; Fat 20 g; Carb 5 g

Instructions

1. In a small bowl, combine the olive oil, minced garlic, lemon juice, lemon zest, dried oregano, salt, and pepper. Mix well.
2. Place the tilapia fillets in a shallow dish or resealable plastic bag.
3. Pour the marinade over the tilapia, ensuring the fillets are well coated.
4. Let the tilapia marinate in the refrigerator for at least 15 minutes.
5. Preheat your air fryer to 375°F (190°C).
6. In a medium bowl, combine the chopped Kalamata olives, chopped green olives, capers, minced garlic, chopped parsley, lemon juice, olive oil, salt, and pepper. Mix well and set aside.
7. Remove the tilapia fillets from the marinade and place them in the air fryer basket in a single layer.
8. Cook for 10-12 minutes, depending on the thickness of the fillets, until the tilapia is cooked through and flakes easily with a fork.
9. Once the tilapia is cooked, remove it from the air fryer and let it rest for a few minutes.
10. Top each fillet with a generous spoonful of olive tapenade.
11. Garnish with fresh parsley and serve with lemon wedges on the side.

 Prep time: 15 min

 Cook time: 12 min

 Servings: 2

Ingredients

- 2 tilapia fillets (about 6 oz each)
- 2 tbsp olive oil
- 2 cloves garlic, minced
- 1 tbsp lemon juice
- 1 tsp lemon zest
- 1 tsp dried oregano
- Salt and pepper to taste
- Fresh parsley for garnish
- Lemon wedges for serving

For the Olive Tapenade:
- 1/2 cup Kalamata olives, pitted and chopped
- 1/4 cup green olives, pitted and chopped
- 2 tbsp capers, drained
- 2 cloves garlic, minced
- 2 tbsp fresh parsley, chopped
- 1 tbsp lemon juice
- 1 tbsp olive oil
- Salt and pepper to taste

Lemon Herb Cod

Cod is a popular white fish known for its mild flavor and firm, flaky texture. It is an excellent source of lean protein and provides essential nutrients such as vitamin B12 and omega-3 fatty acids. The combination of lemon, garlic, and herbs in this recipe enhances the natural flavor of the cod, making it a light and refreshing dish. Air frying the cod ensures that it remains moist and tender while developing a slightly crispy exterior. This lemon herb cod is a quick, healthy, and delicious meal that can be enjoyed any night of the week.

Nutrition   Cal 300; Protein 30 g; Fat 15 g; Carb 2 g

Instructions

1. In a small bowl, combine the olive oil, minced garlic, lemon juice, lemon zest, dried oregano, dried thyme, salt, and pepper. Mix well.
2. Place the cod fillets in a shallow dish or resealable plastic bag.
3. Pour the marinade over the cod, ensuring the fillets are well coated.
4. Let the cod marinate in the refrigerator for at least 15 minutes.
5. Preheat your air fryer to 375°F (190°C).
6. Remove the cod fillets from the marinade and place them in the air fryer basket in a single layer.
7. Cook for 8-10 minutes, depending on the thickness of the fillets, until the cod is cooked through and flakes easily with a fork.
8. Once the cod is cooked, remove it from the air fryer and let it rest for a few minutes.
9. Garnish with fresh parsley.
10. Serve with lemon wedges on the side.

 Prep time: 15 min

 Cook time: 10 min

 Servings: 2

Ingredients

- 2 cod fillets (about 6 oz each)
- 2 tbsp olive oil
- 2 cloves garlic, minced
- 1 tbsp fresh lemon juice
- 1 tsp lemon zest
- 1 tsp dried oregano
- 1 tsp dried thyme
- Salt and pepper to taste
- Fresh parsley for garnish
- Lemon wedges for serving

Herb Fish Cakes

Fish cakes are a versatile and popular dish found in many cuisines around the world. They can be made with various types of fish and a combination of herbs and seasonings to enhance their flavor. This recipe uses fresh herbs like parsley and dill, which are common in Mediterranean cuisine, to add a vibrant and aromatic touch to the fish cakes. Air frying the fish cakes ensures they are crispy on the outside while keeping the inside moist and flavorful. This healthy and delicious dish can be enjoyed as an appetizer, a main course, or even in a sandwich.

Nutrition   Cal 250; Protein 20 g; Fat 10 g; Carb 20 g

Instructions

1. In a large bowl, combine the flaked fish, mashed potatoes, finely chopped red onion, minced garlic, chopped parsley, chopped dill, lemon zest, lemon juice, lightly beaten egg, salt, and pepper. Mix well until all ingredients are evenly incorporated.
2. Divide the mixture into equal portions and shape each portion into patties, about 1 inch thick. This recipe should make about 8 fish cakes.
3. Place the panko breadcrumbs in a shallow dish.
4. Press each fish cake into the breadcrumbs, coating both sides evenly.
5. Preheat your air fryer to 375°F (190°C).
6. Lightly spray the air fryer basket with olive oil spray.
7. Place the fish cakes in the air fryer basket in a single layer, ensuring they do not touch.
8. Lightly spray the tops of the fish cakes with olive oil spray.
9. Cook for 12-15 minutes, flipping halfway through, until the fish cakes are golden brown and crispy.
10. Once the fish cakes are cooked, remove them from the air fryer and let them cool slightly.
11. Serve the fish cakes with tartar sauce or garlic aioli, lemon wedges, and garnish with fresh parsley.

 Prep time: 20 min

 Cook time: 15 min

 Servings: 2

Ingredients

- 1 lb white fish fillets (such as cod or haddock), cooked and flaked
- 1 cup mashed potatoes
- 1/4 cup red onion, finely chopped
- 2 cloves garlic, minced
- 1/4 cup fresh parsley, chopped
- 1/4 cup fresh dill, chopped
- 1 tsp lemon zest
- 1 tbsp fresh lemon juice
- 1 egg, lightly beaten
- 1/2 cup panko breadcrumbs
- Salt and pepper to taste
- Olive oil spray

For Serving:
- Tartar sauce or garlic aioli
- Lemon wedges
- Fresh parsley for garnish

Stuffed Squid

Stuffed squid is a popular dish in Mediterranean cuisine, often enjoyed as an appetizer or a main course. The combination of rice or quinoa, shrimp, and flavorful ingredients like olives and sun-dried tomatoes creates a delicious and hearty filling. Air frying the squid ensures it is cooked perfectly, with a tender interior and a slightly crispy exterior. This method also uses less oil than traditional frying, making it a healthier option. The addition of lemon wedges adds a refreshing citrus note that complements the rich flavors of the stuffing, making this dish a delightful and elegant meal.

Nutrition Cal 250; Protein 20 g; Fat 12 g; Carb 15 g

Instructions

1. In a large bowl, combine the cooked rice or quinoa, finely chopped shrimp, red onion, minced garlic, chopped parsley, Kalamata olives, sun-dried tomatoes, olive oil, dried oregano, lemon zest, salt, and pepper. Mix well until all ingredients are evenly incorporated.
2. Carefully stuff each squid tube with the prepared filling, using a small spoon. Fill each tube about three-quarters full to allow space for the filling to expand.
3. Secure the open end of each squid tube with a toothpick.
4. Preheat your air fryer to 375°F (190°C).
5. Lightly brush the stuffed squid tubes with olive oil.
6. Place the stuffed squid in the air fryer basket in a single layer.
7. Cook for 15-20 minutes, turning halfway through, until the squid is cooked through and slightly crispy on the outside.
8. Once cooked, remove the stuffed squid from the air fryer and let them cool slightly.
9. Garnish with fresh parsley and serve with lemon wedges on the side.

 Prep time: 25 min

 Cook time: 20 min

 Servings: 2

Ingredients

For the Stuffing:
- 1 cup cooked rice or quinoa
- 1/2 cup shrimp, finely chopped
- 1/4 cup red onion, finely chopped
- 2 cloves garlic, minced
- 1/4 cup fresh parsley, chopped
- 1/4 cup Kalamata olives, chopped
- 1/4 cup sun-dried tomatoes, chopped
- 2 tbsp olive oil
- 1 tsp dried oregano
- 1 tsp lemon zest
- Salt and pepper to taste

For the Squid:
- 8 medium-sized squid tubes, cleaned
- 2 tbsp olive oil
- Lemon wedges for serving
- Fresh parsley for garnish

Shrimp and Feta Orzo

Orzo is a type of pasta shaped like large grains of rice, commonly used in Mediterranean cuisine. It is versatile and pairs well with a variety of ingredients. This dish combines the light and fresh flavors of shrimp, tomatoes, and herbs with the creamy, tangy taste of feta cheese. Air frying the shrimp ensures they are perfectly cooked and adds a slight crispness to them. This shrimp and feta orzo is a delicious and healthy meal that captures the essence of Mediterranean cooking, making it a perfect option for a quick and flavorful dinner.

Nutrition Cal 450; Protein 30 g; Fat 20 g; Carb 40 g

Instructions

1. Bring a pot of salted water to a boil. Add the orzo and cook according to the package instructions until al dente. Drain and set aside.
2. In a bowl, combine the shrimp, 1 tbsp olive oil, minced garlic, salt, and pepper. Toss to coat the shrimp evenly.
3. Preheat your air fryer to 375°F (190°C).
4. Place the shrimp in the air fryer basket in a single layer. Cook for 5-7 minutes, turning halfway through, until the shrimp are pink and cooked through. Remove from the air fryer and set aside.
5. In a large skillet, heat the remaining 1 tbsp of olive oil over medium heat.
6. Add the finely chopped red onion and sauté until softened, about 3 minutes.
7. Add the cherry tomatoes, Kalamata olives, and sun-dried tomatoes. Cook for another 3-4 minutes until the tomatoes start to soften.
8. Add the cooked orzo to the skillet with the vegetables and stir to combine.
9. Stir in the cooked shrimp, crumbled feta cheese, chopped parsley, chopped dill, lemon juice, and lemon zest. Mix well and cook for another 2 minutes until everything is heated through.
10. Divide the shrimp and feta orzo between two plates.
11. Garnish with fresh parsley or dill and serve with lemon wedges on the side.

 Prep time: 15 min

 Cook time: 15 min

 Servings: 2

Ingredients

- 1 cup orzo pasta
- 1/2 lb shrimp, peeled and deveined
- 2 tbsp olive oil
- 2 cloves garlic, minced
- 1/4 cup red onion, finely chopped
- 1 cup cherry tomatoes, halved
- 1/4 cup Kalamata olives, pitted and sliced
- 1/4 cup sun-dried tomatoes, chopped
- 1/2 cup feta cheese, crumbled
- 1 tbsp fresh parsley, chopped
- 1 tbsp fresh dill, chopped
- 1 tbsp fresh lemon juice
- 1 tsp lemon zest
- Salt and pepper to taste
- Fresh parsley or dill for garnish
- Lemon wedges for serving

Fish Tacos with Yogurt Sauce

Fish tacos are a staple of coastal Mexican cuisine, known for their fresh and vibrant flavors. This air-fried version offers a healthier take on traditional fried fish tacos by using less oil while still achieving a crispy texture. The yogurt sauce adds a creamy and tangy element that complements the spiced fish and fresh vegetables, making these tacos a delicious and nutritious meal. Perfect for a quick dinner or a casual gathering, these fish tacos bring a taste of the coast to your kitchen.

Nutrition Cal 350; Protein 25 g; Fat 15 g; Carb 30 g

Instructions

1. In a bowl, combine the olive oil, chili powder, cumin, smoked paprika, garlic powder, onion powder, salt, and pepper. Mix well.
2. Add the fish strips to the bowl and toss to coat them evenly with the spice mixture. Let them marinate for at least 15 minutes.
3. 2.Preheat the Air Fryer:
4. Preheat your air fryer to 375°F (190°C).
5. Lightly spray the air fryer basket with olive oil spray.
6. Place the fish strips in the air fryer basket in a single layer.
7. Cook for 8-10 minutes, turning halfway through, until the fish is cooked through and slightly crispy.
8. In a small bowl, combine the Greek yogurt, lime juice, lime zest, minced garlic, chopped cilantro, salt, and pepper. Mix well and refrigerate until ready to use.
9. While the fish is cooking, warm the tortillas in the air fryer for 1-2 minutes or until soft and pliable.
10. Place a few pieces of fish on each tortilla.
11. Top with shredded red cabbage, cherry tomatoes, red onion slices, and avocado slices.
12. Drizzle with the yogurt sauce.
13. Garnish with fresh cilantro.
14. Serve the tacos immediately with lime wedges on the side.

 Prep time: 20 min

 Cook time: 10 min

 Servings: 2

Ingredients

- 1 lb white fish fillets (such as cod or tilapia), cut into strips
- 2 tbsp olive oil
- 1 tsp chili powder
- 1 tsp cumin
- 1/2 tsp smoked paprika
- 1/2 tsp garlic powder
- 1/2 tsp onion powder
- Salt and pepper to taste
- Olive oil spray

For the Yogurt Sauce:
- 1/2 cup Greek yogurt
- 1 tbsp lime juice
- 1 tsp lime zest
- 1 clove garlic, minced
- 1 tbsp fresh cilantro, chopped
- Salt and pepper to taste

For the Tacos:
- 8 small corn or flour tortillas
- 1 cup shredded red cabbage
- 1/2 cup cherry tomatoes, halved
- 1/2 red onion, thinly sliced
- 1 avocado, sliced
- Fresh cilantro for garnish
- Lime wedges for servin

VEGETABLES

Mediterranean Veggie Nuggets

These Mediterranean veggie nuggets are a delicious and healthy alternative to traditional meat nuggets, packed with nutritious vegetables and chickpeas. The combination of fresh herbs like parsley and basil, along with the tangy flavor of Parmesan cheese, gives these nuggets a unique and flavorful twist. Air frying ensures they are crispy on the outside while remaining tender and moist inside. These nuggets are perfect for a snack, appetizer, or even a light meal, and they pair wonderfully with tzatziki sauce or hummus for dipping.

Nutrition Cal 250; Protein 10 g; Fat 10 g; Carb 30 g

Instructions

1. In a large bowl, combine the mashed chickpeas, grated zucchini, grated carrots, chopped red bell pepper, finely chopped red onion, minced garlic, chopped parsley, chopped basil, dried oregano, and ground cumin. Mix well.
2. Stir in the breadcrumbs, grated Parmesan cheese, and lightly beaten egg. Mix until all ingredients are well incorporated. Season with salt and pepper to taste.
3. Take about 1-2 tablespoons of the mixture and shape it into small nugget-sized patties. Place them on a plate or baking sheet.
4. Preheat your air fryer to 375°F (190°C).
5. Lightly spray the air fryer basket with olive oil spray.
6. Place the veggie nuggets in the air fryer basket in a single layer, ensuring they do not touch.
7. Lightly spray the tops of the nuggets with olive oil spray.
8. Cook for 12-15 minutes, turning halfway through, until the nuggets are golden brown and crispy.
9. Once cooked, remove the veggie nuggets from the air fryer and let them cool slightly.
10. Serve with tzatziki sauce or hummus and lemon wedges on the side.

 Prep time: 25 min

 Cook time: 15 min

 Servings: 4

Ingredients

- 1 cup chickpeas, cooked and mashed
- 1 cup zucchini, grated and excess water squeezed out
- 1/2 cup carrots, grated
- 1/2 cup red bell pepper, finely chopped
- 1/4 cup red onion, finely chopped
- 2 cloves garlic, minced
- 1/4 cup fresh parsley, chopped
- 1/4 cup fresh basil, chopped
- 1 tsp dried oregano
- 1 tsp ground cumin
- 1/2 cup breadcrumbs (use gluten-free if needed)
- 1/2 cup grated Parmesan cheese
- 1 egg, lightly beaten
- Salt and pepper to taste
- Olive oil spray

Sweet Potato and Chickpea Patties

Sweet potatoes and chickpeas are both nutrient-dense foods, providing a good source of fiber, vitamins, and minerals. Combining them in these patties creates a delicious and healthy dish that is both satisfying and flavorful. The addition of fresh herbs and spices gives these patties a Mediterranean flair, while air frying ensures they are crispy on the outside and tender on the inside. These patties are perfect for a light meal or a tasty appetizer, especially when paired with a tangy tzatziki or yogurt sauce.

Nutrition   Cal 230; Protein 6 g; Fat 6 g; Carb 38 g

Instructions

1. In a large bowl, combine the mashed sweet potato, mashed chickpeas, finely chopped red onion, minced garlic, chopped parsley, chopped cilantro, ground cumin, ground coriander, and smoked paprika. Mix well.
2. Stir in the breadcrumbs and lightly beaten egg. Mix until all ingredients are well incorporated. Season with salt and pepper to taste.
3. Take about 2 tablespoons of the mixture and shape it into small patties. Place them on a plate or baking sheet.
4. Preheat your air fryer to 375°F (190°C).
5. Lightly spray the air fryer basket with olive oil spray.
6. Place the patties in the air fryer basket in a single layer, ensuring they do not touch.
7. Lightly spray the tops of the patties with olive oil spray.
8. Cook for 12-15 minutes, turning halfway through, until the patties are golden brown and crispy.
9. Once cooked, remove the patties from the air fryer and let them cool slightly.
10. Serve with tzatziki sauce or yogurt sauce and lemon wedges on the side.

 Prep time: 20 min

 Cook time: 15 min

 Servings: 4

Ingredients

- 1 cup sweet potato, cooked and mashed
- 1 cup chickpeas, cooked and mashed
- 1/2 cup red onion, finely chopped
- 2 cloves garlic, minced
- 1/4 cup fresh parsley, chopped
- 1/4 cup fresh cilantro, chopped
- 1 tsp ground cumin
- 1 tsp ground coriander
- 1/2 tsp smoked paprika
- 1/4 cup breadcrumbs (use gluten-free if needed)
- 1 egg, lightly beaten
- Salt and pepper to taste
- Olive oil spray

Vegan Spanakopita

Spanakopita is a traditional Greek pastry that is typically filled with spinach and feta cheese, wrapped in layers of crispy phyllo dough. This vegan version uses crumbled tofu as a substitute for feta cheese, providing a similar texture and protein boost. The fresh herbs and lemon juice add a bright, tangy flavor to the filling. Air frying the spanakopita ensures they are perfectly crispy without the need for excessive oil, making this a healthier alternative to the traditional method. These vegan spanakopita triangles are perfect as an appetizer or snack, bringing a taste of Greece to your kitchen.

Nutrition   Cal 250; Protein 6 g; Fat 15 g; Carb 25 g

Instructions

1. In a large skillet, heat 1 tbsp of olive oil over medium heat.
2. Add the chopped green onions and garlic, and sauté until fragrant, about 2-3 minutes.
3. Add the chopped spinach and cook until wilted (if using fresh) or heated through (if using frozen), about 3-5 minutes.
4. Remove from heat and stir in the chopped dill, parsley, crumbled tofu, lemon juice, salt, and pepper. Mix well and let it cool slightly.
5. Preheat your air fryer to 350°F (175°C).
6. On a clean surface, lay out one sheet of phyllo dough and brush it lightly with olive oil or melted vegan butter.
7. Place another sheet on top and brush it with olive oil as well. Repeat this process until you have four layers.
8. Cut the layered phyllo into 3-inch wide strips.
9. Place a tablespoon of the spinach mixture at one end of each strip.
10. Fold the corner of the phyllo over the filling to form a triangle. Continue folding the strip in a triangle pattern until you reach the end.
11. Brush the outside of each triangle with olive oil.
12. Repeat with the remaining phyllo sheets and filling.
13. Place the spanakopita triangles in the air fryer basket in a single layer.
14. Cook for 10-15 minutes, until the phyllo is golden brown and crispy.
15. Once cooked, remove the spanakopita from the air fryer and let them cool slightly before serving.

 Prep time: 25 min

 Cook time: 15 min

 Servings: 4

Ingredients

For the Filling:
- 1 lb fresh spinach, washed and chopped (or 10 oz frozen spinach, thawed and drained)
- 1/2 cup green onions, finely chopped
- 1/4 cup fresh dill, chopped
- 1/4 cup fresh parsley, chopped
- 1/2 cup firm tofu, crumbled
- 2 cloves garlic, minced
- 1 tbsp olive oil
- 1 tbsp lemon juice
- Salt and pepper to taste

For the Pastry:
- 8 sheets phyllo dough, thawed
- 1/4 cup olive oil or melted vegan butter for brushing

Asparagus with Almond Crumbs

Asparagus is a nutrient-dense vegetable that is rich in vitamins A, C, and K, as well as folate and fiber. It has been enjoyed for centuries for its unique flavor and health benefits. The addition of almond crumbs not only adds a delightful crunch to the dish but also boosts its nutritional value with healthy fats and protein from the almonds. Air frying the asparagus ensures a crispy texture without the need for excessive oil, making this dish a healthy and delicious side that pairs well with a variety of main courses.

Nutrition Cal 150; Protein 4 g; Fat 12 g; Carb 8 g

Instructions

1. Wash and trim the asparagus spears, cutting off the woody ends.
2. In a bowl, combine the almond crumbs, panko breadcrumbs, minced garlic, lemon zest, salt, and black pepper. Mix well.
3. Lightly coat the asparagus spears with olive oil.
4. Roll each asparagus spear in the almond crumb mixture, pressing gently to adhere the crumbs to the asparagus.
5. Preheat your air fryer to 375°F (190°C).
6. Place the coated asparagus spears in the air fryer basket in a single layer. You may need to cook in batches depending on the size of your air fryer.
7. Cook for 8-10 minutes, shaking the basket halfway through, until the asparagus is tender and the almond crumbs are golden brown.
8. Once cooked, remove the asparagus from the air fryer and transfer to a serving plate.
9. Garnish with fresh parsley, if using.
10. Serve with lemon wedges on the side for an extra burst of flavor.

 Prep time: 10 min

 Cook time: 10 min

 Servings: 4

Ingredients

- 1 lb asparagus, trimmed
- 2 tbsp olive oil
- 1/2 cup almond crumbs (finely chopped almonds or almond flour)
- 1/4 cup panko breadcrumbs (use gluten-free if needed)
- 2 cloves garlic, minced
- 1 tsp lemon zest
- 1/2 tsp salt
- 1/4 tsp black pepper
- 1 tbsp fresh parsley, chopped (optional for garnish)
- Lemon wedges for serving

Vegan Mushroom Gyros

Gyros are a popular Greek street food traditionally made with meat cooked on a vertical rotisserie. This vegan version uses mushrooms as a hearty and flavorful substitute, providing a similar texture and umami taste. The homemade tzatziki sauce adds a creamy and tangy element, perfectly complementing the spiced mushrooms. Air frying the mushrooms ensures they are cooked to perfection with minimal oil, making these vegan mushroom gyros a healthy and delicious alternative to the classic dish.

Nutrition   Cal 300; Protein 8 g; Fat 15 g; Carb 35 g

Instructions

1. In a large bowl, combine the sliced mushrooms, olive oil, minced garlic, smoked paprika, ground cumin, dried oregano, ground coriander, salt, and pepper. Toss to coat the mushrooms evenly with the spices.
2. Preheat your air fryer to 375°F (190°C).
3. Place the seasoned mushrooms in the air fryer basket in a single layer.
4. Cook for 10-15 minutes, shaking the basket halfway through, until the mushrooms are tender and slightly crispy.
5. In a medium bowl, combine the coconut yogurt, grated cucumber, minced garlic, chopped dill, lemon juice, salt, and pepper. Mix well and refrigerate until ready to use.
6. While the mushrooms are cooking, warm the pita breads in the air fryer for 1-2 minutes or until soft and pliable.
7. Place a generous portion of the cooked mushrooms on each pita bread.
8. Top with shredded lettuce, cherry tomatoes, red onion slices, and Kalamata olives.
9. Drizzle with tzatziki sauce.
10. Garnish with fresh parsley and serve immediately.

 Prep time: 20 min

 Cook time: 15 min

 Servings: 2

Ingredients

For the Mushroom Filling:
- 1 lb mushrooms (such as portobello or cremini), sliced
- 2 tbsp olive oil
- 2 cloves garlic, minced
- 1 tsp smoked paprika
- 1 tsp ground cumin
- 1 tsp dried oregano
- 1/2 tsp ground coriander

For the Tzatziki Sauce:
- 1 cup coconut yogurt or any vegan yogurt
- 1/2 cucumber, grated and excess water squeezed out
- 1 clove garlic, minced
- 1 tbsp fresh dill, chopped
- 1 tbsp fresh lemon juice

For Assembly:
- 4 pita breads or flatbreads (use gluten-free if needed)
- 1 cup shredded lettuce
- 1/2 cup cherry tomatoes, halved
- 1/4 red onion, thinly sliced
- 1/4 cup Kalamata olives, pitted and halved

Stuffed Artichokes with Lemon and Herbs

Artichokes have been enjoyed since ancient times and are particularly popular in Mediterranean cuisine. They are packed with antioxidants, fiber, and vitamins, making them a nutritious addition to any meal. This stuffed artichoke recipe combines fresh herbs and lemon for a flavorful and aromatic dish. Air frying the artichokes ensures they are tender on the inside and slightly crispy on the outside, while the stuffing adds a deliciously savory element. This dish is perfect as an appetizer or a side dish and brings a taste of Mediterranean elegance to your table.

Nutrition   Cal 250; Protein 8 g; Fat 16 g; Carb 22 g

Instructions

1. Fill a large bowl with cold water and squeeze the juice of one lemon into the water.
2. Trim the tops off the artichokes and snip the tips of the leaves with kitchen scissors.
3. Remove the small outer leaves near the base and rub the cut parts with a halved lemon to prevent browning.
4. Cut the artichokes in half lengthwise and remove the choke (the fuzzy part) with a spoon. Place the cleaned artichokes in the lemon water to prevent browning.
5. In a medium bowl, combine the breadcrumbs, grated vegan Parmesan cheese, minced garlic, chopped parsley, chopped dill, chopped mint, olive oil, lemon zest, salt, and pepper. Mix well.
6. Drain the artichokes and pat them dry.
7. Spoon the stuffing mixture into the center and between the leaves of each artichoke half, pressing gently to adhere.
8. Preheat your air fryer to 375°F (190°C).
9. Lightly spray the air fryer basket with olive oil spray.
10. Place the stuffed artichokes in the air fryer basket in a single layer.
11. Cook for 15-20 minutes, until the artichokes are tender and the stuffing is golden brown.
12. In a small bowl, whisk together the olive oil, lemon juice, minced garlic, salt, and pepper.
13. Once the artichokes are cooked, remove them from the air fryer and drizzle with the lemon and garlic mixture.

 Prep time: 30 min

 Cook time: 20 min

 Servings: 4

Ingredients

- 4 large artichokes
- 1 lemon, halved (for rubbing the artichokes to prevent browning)
- 1 cup breadcrumbs (use gluten-free if needed)
- 1/2 cup grated vegan Parmesan cheese
- 2 cloves garlic, minced
- 1/4 cup fresh parsley, chopped
- 2 tbsp fresh dill, chopped
- 2 tbsp fresh mint, chopped
- 2 tbsp olive oil
- 1 tsp lemon zest
- Salt and pepper to taste

For the Drizzle:
- 1/4 cup olive oil
- 2 tbsp fresh lemon juice
- 1 clove garlic, minced
- Salt and pepper to taste

Quinoa and Black Bean Stuffed Peppers

Stuffed peppers are a versatile dish found in many cuisines worldwide, from Mediterranean to Mexican. This version uses quinoa, a nutrient-rich grain that is high in protein and fiber, making it a healthy and filling option. The combination of black beans, corn, and spices adds a southwestern flair, while air frying ensures the peppers are perfectly cooked with a slight char. These quinoa and black bean stuffed peppers are a delicious and nutritious meal that can be enjoyed as a main course or a hearty side dish.

Nutrition   Cal 300; Protein 10 g; Fat 10 g; Carb 45 g

Instructions

1. In a large bowl, combine the cooked quinoa, black beans, corn kernels, finely chopped red onion, minced garlic, cherry tomatoes, chopped cilantro, ground cumin, smoked paprika, chili powder, salt, and pepper. Mix well.
2. Lightly coat the inside of each bell pepper with olive oil.
3. Spoon the quinoa and black bean mixture into each bell pepper, packing it tightly. If using, top each stuffed pepper with a sprinkle of vegan cheese or shredded cheese.
4. Preheat your air fryer to 375°F (190°C).
5. Place the stuffed peppers in the air fryer basket in a single layer.
6. Cook for 12-15 minutes, until the peppers are tender and the tops are slightly browned. If using cheese, it should be melted and bubbly.
7. Once cooked, remove the stuffed peppers from the air fryer.
8. Garnish with additional chopped cilantro if desired and serve with fresh lime wedges on the side.

 Prep time: 20 min

 Cook time: 15 min

 Servings: 4

Ingredients

- 4 large bell peppers (any color), tops cut off and seeds removed
- 1 cup cooked quinoa
- 1 cup black beans, cooked and drained
- 1/2 cup corn kernels (fresh, frozen, or canned)
- 1/2 cup red onion, finely chopped
- 2 cloves garlic, minced
- 1 cup cherry tomatoes, halved
- 1/4 cup fresh cilantro, chopped
- 1 tsp ground cumin
- 1 tsp smoked paprika
- 1 tsp chili powder
- Salt and pepper to taste
- 1/2 cup vegan cheese or shredded cheese (optional)
- 2 tbsp olive oil
- Fresh lime wedges for serving

Vegan Moussaka

Moussaka is a traditional Greek dish typically made with layers of eggplant, ground meat, and a creamy bechamel sauce. This vegan version substitutes lentils for the meat, providing a hearty and protein-rich filling. The use of nutritional yeast in the bechamel sauce adds a cheesy flavor while keeping the dish dairy-free. Air frying the eggplant ensures it is tender and slightly caramelized without the need for excessive oil, making this vegan moussaka a healthier but equally delicious alternative to the classic recipe.

Nutrition Cal 350; Protein 12 g; Fat 15 g; Carb 40 g

Instructions

1. Preheat your air fryer to 375°F (190°C).
2. Brush the eggplant slices with olive oil and season with salt and pepper.
3. Place the eggplant slices in the air fryer basket in a single layer. Cook for 10-12 minutes, flipping halfway through, until they are tender and slightly browned. You may need to do this in batches. Set aside.
4. In a large skillet, heat 2 tbsp of olive oil over medium heat.
5. Add the finely chopped onion and minced garlic, and sauté until softened, about 3-4 minutes.
6. Add the chopped mushrooms and cook for another 3-4 minutes until they release their moisture and start to brown.
7. Stir in the cooked lentils, diced tomatoes, red wine (if using), ground cinnamon, ground allspice, dried oregano, salt, and pepper. Simmer for 10-15 minutes until the mixture thickens and the flavors meld. Remove from heat and set aside.
8. In a medium saucepan, heat 2 tbsp of olive oil over medium heat.
9. Whisk in the flour and cook for 1-2 minutes to form a roux.
10. Gradually add the almond milk, whisking continuously to avoid lumps.
11. Cook until the sauce thickens, about 5-7 minutes.
12. Stir in the nutritional yeast, nutmeg, salt, and pepper. Remove from heat.
13. Preheat your oven to 375°F (190°C).
14. In a baking dish, layer half of the eggplant slices on the bottom.
15. Spread the lentil filling evenly over the eggplant.
16. Top with the remaining eggplant slices.
17. Pour the bechamel sauce over the top layer of eggplant, spreading it evenly.
18. Bake in the preheated oven for 25-30 minutes, until the top is golden brown and the moussaka is heated through.
19. Once baked, let the moussaka cool for a few minutes before slicing.
20. Serve warm, garnished with fresh herbs if desired.

 Prep time: 30 min

 Cook time: 45 min

 Servings: 4

Ingredients

- 2 large eggplants, sliced into 1/4-inch rounds
- 2 tbsp olive oil

For the Filling:
- 1 cup lentils, cooked and drained
- 1 can (14.5 oz) diced tomatoes
- 1/2 cup onion, finely chopped
- 2 cloves garlic, minced
- 1/2 cup mushrooms, chopped
- 1/4 cup red wine (optional)
- 1 tsp ground cinnamon
- 1 tsp ground allspice
- 1 tsp dried oregano
- Salt and pepper to taste
- 2 tbsp olive oil

For the Bechamel Sauce:
- 2 tbsp olive oil
- 2 tbsp all-purpose flour (use gluten-free if needed)
- 2 cups unsweetened almond milk
- 1/4 cup nutritional yeast
- 1/4 tsp nutmeg

Broccoli with Garlic and Parmesan

Broccoli is a nutrient-dense vegetable packed with vitamins C and K, fiber, and antioxidants. Air frying broccoli is a quick and healthy way to cook it, preserving its nutrients while adding a delightful crispiness. The combination of garlic and Parmesan adds a rich, savory flavor, while the lemon zest brightens up the dish. This air-fried broccoli makes a perfect side dish for any meal, providing a delicious way to enjoy this versatile vegetable.

Nutrition   Cal 120; Protein 4 g; Fat 9 g; Carb 8 g

Instructions

1. Wash and dry the broccoli florets.
2. In a large bowl, combine the broccoli florets, olive oil, minced garlic, salt, and pepper. Toss to coat evenly.
3. Preheat your air fryer to 375°F (190°C).
4. Place the seasoned broccoli florets in the air fryer basket in a single layer.
5. Cook for 8-10 minutes, shaking the basket halfway through, until the broccoli is tender and slightly crispy on the edges.
6. Remove the broccoli from the air fryer and transfer it back to the bowl.
7. Immediately sprinkle the grated Parmesan cheese and lemon zest over the hot broccoli. Toss to coat evenly.
8. Transfer the broccoli to a serving platter.
9. Garnish with fresh parsley if desired.
10. Serve with lemon wedges on the side for an extra burst of flavor.

 Prep time: 10 min

 Cook time: 10 min

 Servings: 4

Ingredients

- o 1 lb broccoli florets
- o 2 tbsp olive oil
- o 3 cloves garlic, minced
- o 1/4 cup grated Parmesan cheese (use vegan Parmesan if needed)
- o 1 tsp lemon zest
- o Salt and pepper to taste
- o Fresh parsley for garnish (optional)
- o Lemon wedges for serving

Cauliflower Steaks with Tahini Drizzle

Cauliflower is a versatile vegetable that can be transformed into various dishes, from rice substitutes to pizza crusts. When cut into steaks and air-fried, it develops a deliciously crispy texture while maintaining its tender interior. The tahini drizzle adds a rich, nutty flavor that complements the smoky spices on the cauliflower. This dish is not only tasty but also packed with nutrients, making it a great option for a healthy and satisfying meal.

Nutrition   Cal 180; Protein 5 g; Fat 14 g; Carb 12 g

Instructions

1. Remove the leaves and trim the stem of the cauliflower, but keep the core intact.
2. Slice the cauliflower into 1-inch thick steaks. You should get about 4-5 steaks from one head.
3. In a small bowl, mix together the olive oil, minced garlic, ground cumin, smoked paprika, salt, and pepper.
4. Brush both sides of the cauliflower steaks with the seasoned olive oil mixture.
5. Preheat your air fryer to 375°F (190°C).
6. 3.Cook the Cauliflower Steaks:
7. Place the cauliflower steaks in the air fryer basket in a single layer. You may need to cook them in batches depending on the size of your air fryer.
8. Cook for 15-20 minutes, flipping halfway through, until the cauliflower is tender and golden brown on the edges.
9. In a small bowl, whisk together the tahini, lemon juice, minced garlic, and a pinch of salt.
10. Gradually add water, one tablespoon at a time, until the sauce reaches a drizzling consistency.
11. Once the cauliflower steaks are cooked, transfer them to a serving platter.
12. Drizzle the tahini sauce over the cauliflower steaks.
13. Garnish with chopped fresh parsley and toasted sesame seeds.
14. Serve with lemon wedges on the side.

 Prep time: 15 min

 Cook time: 20 min

 Servings: 4

Ingredients

- 1 large head of cauliflower
- 3 tbsp olive oil
- 2 cloves garlic, minced
- 1 tsp ground cumin
- 1 tsp smoked paprika
- Salt and pepper to taste

For the Tahini Drizzle:
- 1/4 cup tahini
- 2 tbsp lemon juice
- 1 clove garlic, minced
- 2-3 tbsp water (to thin the sauce)
- Salt to taste

For Garnish:
- 1 tbsp fresh parsley, chopped
- 1 tbsp toasted sesame seeds
- Lemon wedges for serving

APPETIZER

Eggplant Rollatini

Eggplant rollatini is a classic Italian dish that features eggplant slices rolled around a creamy cheese filling and baked in marinara sauce. This dish is a delicious and lighter alternative to traditional pasta-based recipes, and using an air fryer for the eggplant slices ensures they are perfectly tender without being overly oily. The combination of ricotta, Parmesan, and mozzarella cheeses creates a rich and flavorful filling, while the marinara sauce adds a tangy and savory element. This air-fried eggplant rollatini is a delightful and satisfying dish that is sure to impress.

Nutrition   Cal 350; Protein 20 g; Fat 20 g; Carb 25 g

Instructions

1. Preheat your air fryer to 375°F (190°C).
2. Brush both sides of the eggplant slices with olive oil and season with salt and pepper.
3. Place the eggplant slices in the air fryer basket in a single layer. You may need to cook them in batches.
4. Cook for 8-10 minutes, flipping halfway through, until the eggplant is tender and slightly golden.
5. In a medium bowl, combine the ricotta cheese, grated Parmesan cheese, shredded mozzarella cheese, chopped basil, minced garlic, lightly beaten egg, salt, and pepper. Mix well until all ingredients are thoroughly combined.
6. Preheat your oven to 375°F (190°C).
7. Spread a thin layer of marinara sauce on the bottom of a baking dish.
8. Place a spoonful of the ricotta filling at one end of each eggplant slice and roll it up tightly.
9. Place the rolled eggplant slices seam-side down in the baking dish.
10. Pour the remaining marinara sauce over the top of the eggplant rolls.
11. Bake in the preheated oven for 20 minutes, until the sauce is bubbly and the cheese is melted.
12. Once cooked, remove the eggplant rollatini from the oven and let them cool slightly.
13. Garnish with additional fresh basil if desired.

 Prep time: 30 min

 Cook time: 15 min

 Servings: 4

Ingredients

- 2 large eggplants, sliced lengthwise into 1/4-inch thick slices
- 2 tbsp olive oil
- Salt and pepper to taste

For the Filling:
- 1 cup ricotta cheese (use vegan ricotta if needed)
- 1/2 cup grated Parmesan cheese (use vegan Parmesan if needed)
- 1 cup shredded mozzarella cheese (use vegan mozzarella if needed)
- 1/4 cup fresh basil, chopped
- 2 cloves garlic, minced
- 1 egg, lightly beaten (or flax egg for vegan)
- Salt and pepper to taste

For the Marinara Sauce:
- 2 cups marinara sauce (store-bought or homemade)

Veggie Chips

Veggie chips are a nutritious alternative to traditional potato chips, offering a variety of vitamins and minerals depending on the vegetables used. Air frying the chips significantly reduces the amount of oil needed, making them a healthier option while still providing that satisfying crunch. The combination of different vegetables not only adds vibrant colors to your snack but also introduces a range of flavors and textures, making these air-fried veggie chips a delicious and wholesome treat.

Nutrition   Cal 120; Protein 2 g; Fat 5 g; Carb 18 g

Instructions

1. Wash and peel the vegetables as needed.
2. Using a mandoline or a sharp knife, slice the zucchini, carrot, beet, and sweet potato into thin, even slices, about 1/8-inch thick.
3. In a large bowl, combine the vegetable slices with olive oil, sea salt, black pepper, paprika, garlic powder, and dried thyme. Toss well to ensure all slices are evenly coated with the seasoning.
4. Preheat your air fryer to 350°F (175°C).
5. Place the seasoned vegetable slices in the air fryer basket in a single layer. You may need to do this in batches depending on the size of your air fryer.
6. Cook for 10-15 minutes, shaking the basket halfway through, until the chips are crispy and golden brown. Keep an eye on them as cooking times may vary depending on the thickness of the slices and the type of vegetable.
7. Once cooked, remove the veggie chips from the air fryer and let them cool on a wire rack. This will help them stay crispy.
8. Serve immediately as a healthy snack or side dish.

 Prep time: 15 min

 Cook time: 15 min

 Servings: 4

Ingredients

- o 1 large zucchini
- o 1 large carrot
- o 1 large beet
- o 1 large sweet potato
- o 2 tbsp olive oil
- o 1 tsp sea salt
- o 1/2 tsp black pepper
- o 1/2 tsp paprika
- o 1/2 tsp garlic powder
- o 1/2 tsp dried thyme

Mushroom Caps with Herb Cheese

Mushrooms are a versatile ingredient that can be used in a variety of dishes. They are low in calories and rich in vitamins, minerals, and antioxidants. Stuffing mushrooms with herb cheese adds a creamy and flavorful element to the dish, making them an elegant appetizer or side dish. Air frying the mushrooms ensures they are perfectly cooked and slightly crispy on the outside, while the filling remains warm and gooey. This simple yet delicious recipe is perfect for entertaining or as a special treat for yourself.

Nutrition Cal 150; Protein 5 g; Fat 12 g; Carb 5 g

Instructions

1. Clean the mushroom caps with a damp paper towel and remove the stems.
2. Brush the mushroom caps with olive oil and season with salt and pepper.
3. In a small bowl, combine the herb cheese, minced garlic, chopped parsley, and chopped chives. Mix until well combined.
4. Fill each mushroom cap with a generous amount of the herb cheese mixture.
5. Preheat your air fryer to 375°F (190°C).
6. Place the stuffed mushroom caps in the air fryer basket in a single layer.
7. Cook for 8-10 minutes, until the mushrooms are tender and the cheese is melted and bubbly.
8. If desired, sprinkle the stuffed mushrooms with grated Parmesan cheese immediately after cooking.
9. Transfer the mushrooms to a serving plate and garnish with additional fresh herbs if desired.

 Prep time: 15 min

 Cook time: 10 min

 Servings: 4

Ingredients

- o 12 large mushroom caps (such as cremini or button mushrooms), stems removed
- o 4 oz herb cheese (such as Boursin or herbed cream cheese)
- o 2 cloves garlic, minced
- o 1 tbsp fresh parsley, chopped
- o 1 tbsp fresh chives, chopped
- o 1 tbsp olive oil
- o Salt and pepper to taste
- o 1/4 cup grated Parmesan cheese (optional for garnish)

Mozzarella Sticks

Mozzarella sticks are a beloved appetizer that originated in the United States, inspired by Italian cuisine. The combination of crispy breadcrumb coating and gooey melted cheese makes them an irresistible treat. Air frying mozzarella sticks significantly reduces the amount of oil needed compared to traditional frying, resulting in a healthier yet still delicious snack. Freezing the coated sticks before cooking is a crucial step to ensure they hold their shape and don't melt too quickly in the air fryer. Enjoy these air-fried mozzarella sticks as a fun and tasty appetizer or snack!

Nutrition Cal 250; Protein 15 g; Fat 15 g; Carb 15 g

Instructions

1. Cut each mozzarella string cheese stick in half to create 16 pieces.
2. Place the flour in a shallow dish.
3. In another shallow dish, beat the eggs.
4. In a third shallow dish, combine the panko breadcrumbs, grated Parmesan cheese, dried Italian seasoning, garlic powder, salt, and pepper.
5. Dredge each piece of mozzarella in the flour, shaking off any excess.
6. Dip into the beaten eggs, allowing any excess to drip off.
7. Roll in the breadcrumb mixture, pressing gently to adhere. For extra crispiness, repeat the egg and breadcrumb coating once more.
8. Place the coated mozzarella sticks on a baking sheet lined with parchment paper.
9. Freeze for at least 1 hour, or until solid. This prevents the cheese from melting too quickly during cooking.
10. Preheat your air fryer to 400°F (200°C).
11. Lightly spray the air fryer basket with olive oil spray.
12. Place the frozen mozzarella sticks in the air fryer basket in a single layer. Lightly spray the tops with olive oil spray.
13. Cook for 6-8 minutes, turning halfway through, until the mozzarella sticks are golden brown and crispy. Keep an eye on them to prevent the cheese from oozing out.
14. Remove the mozzarella sticks from the air fryer and let them cool for a minute.
15. Serve warm with marinara sauce for dipping.

 Prep time: 15 min

 Cook time: 8 min

 Servings: 4

Ingredients

- 8 mozzarella string cheese sticks
- 1/2 cup all-purpose flour (use gluten-free flour if needed)
- 2 large eggs, beaten
- 1 cup panko breadcrumbs (use gluten-free breadcrumbs if needed)
- 1/2 cup grated Parmesan cheese
- 1 tsp dried Italian seasoning
- 1 tsp garlic powder
- Salt and pepper to taste
- Olive oil spray

For Serving:
- Marinara sauce

Feta Cheese Bites

Feta cheese, a staple in Mediterranean cuisine, is known for its tangy flavor and crumbly texture. These air-fried feta cheese bites offer a delightful combination of crispy coating and creamy interior, making them a perfect appetizer or snack. Using the air fryer significantly reduces the amount of oil needed compared to traditional frying methods, keeping the dish light and healthy. Serving these bites with a drizzle of honey enhances the savory-sweet contrast, while marinara sauce provides a tangy complement. This recipe is a delicious way to enjoy the flavors of the Mediterranean diet.

Nutrition   Cal 200; Protein 8 g; Fat 12 g; Carb 12 g

Instructions

1. Cut the block of feta cheese into 1-inch cubes.
2. Place the flour in a shallow dish.
3. In another shallow dish, beat the eggs.
4. In a third shallow dish, combine the panko breadcrumbs, dried oregano, dried thyme, garlic powder, salt, and pepper.
5. Dredge each feta cheese cube in the flour, shaking off any excess.
6. Dip into the beaten eggs, allowing any excess to drip off.
7. Roll in the breadcrumb mixture, pressing gently to adhere. For extra crispiness, repeat the egg and breadcrumb coating once more.
8. Place the coated feta cheese cubes on a baking sheet lined with parchment paper.
9. Freeze for at least 30 minutes. This helps the coating adhere and prevents the cheese from melting too quickly during cooking.
10. Preheat your air fryer to 375°F (190°C).
11. Lightly spray the air fryer basket with olive oil spray.
12. Place the frozen feta cheese bites in the air fryer basket in a single layer. Lightly spray the tops with olive oil spray.
13. Cook for 8-10 minutes, turning halfway through, until the bites are golden brown and crispy.
14. Remove the feta cheese bites from the air fryer and let them cool for a minute.
15. Garnish with fresh parsley or mint.
16. Serve warm with a drizzle of honey or a side of marinara sauce.

 Prep time: 15 min

 Cook time: 10 min

 Servings: 4

Ingredients

- o 8 oz block of feta cheese, cut into 1-inch cubes
- o 1/2 cup all-purpose flour (use gluten-free flour if needed)
- o 2 large eggs, beaten
- o 1 cup panko breadcrumbs (use gluten-free breadcrumbs if needed)
- o 1 tsp dried oregano
- o 1 tsp dried thyme
- o 1 tsp garlic powder
- o Salt and pepper to taste
- o Olive oil spray

For Serving:
- o Honey or marinara sauce
- o Fresh parsley or mint for garnish

Air-Fried Ravioli

Ravioli, a traditional Italian pasta, can be transformed into a crispy appetizer or snack by air frying. This method requires significantly less oil than deep frying, making it a healthier option that retains all the delicious flavors and textures. The whole wheat breadcrumbs add a nutty flavor and extra fiber, aligning with the principles of the Mediterranean diet. Serving air-fried ravioli with marinara sauce provides a tangy complement that enhances the overall taste, making it a perfect dish for entertaining or as a unique meal option.

Nutrition Cal 300; Protein 10 g; Fat 10 g; Carb 40 g

Instructions

1. If using frozen ravioli, cook according to package instructions until just tender. Drain and let cool slightly.
2. In a shallow dish, combine the whole wheat breadcrumbs, grated Parmesan cheese, dried oregano, dried basil, garlic powder, and smoked paprika.
3. In another shallow dish, beat the eggs.
4. Dip each ravioli into the beaten eggs, allowing any excess to drip off.
5. Roll in the breadcrumb mixture, pressing gently to adhere. Ensure each ravioli is well coated.
6. Preheat your air fryer to 375°F (190°C).
7. Lightly spray the air fryer basket with olive oil spray.
8. Place the breaded ravioli in the air fryer basket in a single layer. Lightly spray the tops with olive oil spray.
9. Cook for 8-10 minutes, turning halfway through, until the ravioli are golden brown and crispy.
10. Remove the ravioli from the air fryer and let them cool for a minute.
11. Serve warm with marinara sauce for dipping and garnish with fresh basil.

 Prep time: 20 min

 Cook time: 10 min

 Servings: 4

Ingredients

- 1 package (9 oz) fresh or frozen cheese ravioli (use whole wheat or gluten-free if needed)
- 1/2 cup whole wheat breadcrumbs (or gluten-free breadcrumbs)
- 1/4 cup grated Parmesan cheese (use vegan Parmesan if needed)
- 1 tsp dried oregano
- 1 tsp dried basil
- 1/2 tsp garlic powder
- 1/2 tsp smoked paprika
- 2 large eggs, beaten
- Olive oil spray

For Serving:
- Marinara sauce
- Fresh basil for garnish

Calamari Rings with Dip

Calamari, a popular dish in Mediterranean cuisine, is typically deep-fried. Air frying provides a healthier alternative by reducing the amount of oil used, resulting in a lighter but still crispy texture. The whole wheat breadcrumbs and Parmesan cheese add a flavorful crunch that complements the tender calamari rings. The lemon garlic aioli, made with Greek yogurt, provides a tangy and creamy dip that enhances the overall taste of the dish. This air-fried calamari is a delicious and healthier way to enjoy a classic Mediterranean appetizer.

Nutrition Cal 280; Protein 20 g; Fat 12 g; Carb 22 g

Instructions

1. Rinse the calamari rings under cold water and pat dry with paper towels.
2. In a shallow dish, place the whole wheat flour.
3. In another shallow dish, beat the eggs.
4. In a third shallow dish, combine the whole wheat breadcrumbs, grated Parmesan cheese, dried oregano, dried basil, garlic powder, salt, and pepper.
5. Dredge each calamari ring in the flour, shaking off any excess.
6. Dip into the beaten eggs, allowing any excess to drip off.
7. Roll in the breadcrumb mixture, pressing gently to adhere. Ensure each ring is well coated.
8. Preheat your air fryer to 400°F (200°C).
9. Lightly spray the air fryer basket with olive oil spray.
10. Place the breaded calamari rings in the air fryer basket in a single layer. Lightly spray the tops with olive oil spray.
11. Cook for 8-10 minutes, turning halfway through, until the calamari rings are golden brown and crispy.

Prepare the Lemon Garlic Aioli:

12. In a small bowl, combine the Greek yogurt, olive oil, minced garlic, lemon juice, lemon zest, salt, and pepper. Mix well and refrigerate until ready to serve.
13. Once the calamari rings are cooked, remove them from the air fryer and let them cool for a minute.
14. Serve warm with the lemon garlic aioli on the side for dipping.

 Prep time: 20 min

 Cook time: 10 min

 Servings: 4

Ingredients

- 1 lb calamari rings (squid rings)
- 1/2 cup whole wheat flour (use gluten-free flour if needed)
- 2 large eggs, beaten
- 1 cup whole wheat breadcrumbs (use gluten-free breadcrumbs if needed)
- 1/4 cup grated Parmesan cheese (use vegan Parmesan if needed)
- 1 tsp dried oregano
- 1 tsp dried basil
- 1/2 tsp garlic powder
- Olive oil spray

For the Lemon Garlic Aioli:

- 1/2 cup Greek yogurt (use vegan yogurt if needed)
- 2 tbsp olive oil
- 1 clove garlic, minced
- 1 tbsp lemon juice
- 1 tsp lemon zest

Greek Salad Nachos

Greek salad nachos offer a fresh and Mediterranean twist on traditional nachos. By using pita chips instead of tortilla chips and topping them with classic Greek salad ingredients, this dish combines the best of both worlds. The homemade tzatziki sauce adds a creamy and tangy element that complements the crunchy pita chips and fresh vegetables. This dish is not only delicious but also a healthier option, perfect for parties, gatherings, or a fun family meal.

Nutrition   Cal 320; Protein 10 g; Fat 18 g; Carb 30 g

Instructions

1. Preheat your air fryer to 375°F (190°C).
2. Cut each pita bread into 8 triangles.
3. In a bowl, combine the olive oil, dried oregano, garlic powder, and salt. Brush the pita triangles with the seasoned olive oil mixture.
4. Place the pita triangles in the air fryer basket in a single layer. You may need to cook them in batches.
5. Cook for 5-7 minutes, shaking the basket halfway through, until the pita chips are golden brown and crispy. Set aside to cool.
6. Arrange the pita chips on a large serving platter.
7. Top with halved cherry tomatoes, diced cucumber, sliced Kalamata olives, thinly sliced red onion, and crumbled feta cheese.
8. Drizzle the tzatziki sauce over the nachos.
9. Garnish with chopped fresh parsley.
10. Serve the Greek salad nachos immediately, either as an appetizer or a light meal.

 Prep time: 15 min

 Cook time: 10 min

 Servings: 4

Ingredients

For the Pita Chips:
- 4 whole wheat pita breads
- 2 tbsp olive oil
- 1 tsp dried oregano
- 1/2 tsp garlic powder
- Salt to taste

For the Toppings:
- 1 cup cherry tomatoes, halved
- 1/2 cup cucumber, diced
- 1/2 cup Kalamata olives, pitted and sliced
- 1/4 cup red onion, thinly sliced
- 1/2 cup feta cheese, crumbled (use vegan feta if needed)
- 1/4 cup fresh parsley, chopped

Roasted Eggplant & Feta Dip

Eggplant is a versatile vegetable commonly used in Mediterranean cuisine. It is low in calories and high in fiber, making it an excellent choice for a healthy diet. Roasting the eggplant enhances its natural sweetness and adds a smoky flavor to the dip. Combined with tangy feta cheese, creamy Greek yogurt, and fresh herbs, this roasted eggplant and feta dip is a delicious and nutritious appetizer that captures the essence of Mediterranean flavors.

Nutrition   Cal 150; Protein 5 g; Fat 10 g; Carb 10 g

Instructions

1. Preheat your air fryer to 375°F (190°C).
2. Cut the eggplant in half lengthwise and score the flesh in a crosshatch pattern. Brush the cut sides with 1 tbsp of olive oil and season with salt and pepper.
3. Place the eggplant halves in the air fryer basket, cut side up. Lightly spray with olive oil.
4. Cook the eggplant in the air fryer for 15-20 minutes, until the flesh is tender and lightly browned.
5. Remove from the air fryer and let it cool slightly.
6. Scoop the roasted eggplant flesh into a mixing bowl, discarding the skin.
7. Add the minced garlic, crumbled feta cheese, Greek yogurt, lemon juice, lemon zest, chopped parsley, and chopped mint.
8. Mash the mixture with a fork or blend it in a food processor until smooth and creamy. Adjust the seasoning with salt and pepper to taste.
9. Transfer the dip to a serving bowl.
10. Drizzle with the remaining 1 tbsp of olive oil and garnish with additional chopped herbs if desired.
11. Serve with pita chips, bread, or fresh vegetables.

 Prep time: 15 min

 Cook time: 20 min

 Servings: 4

Ingredients

- 1 large eggplant
- 2 tbsp olive oil
- 3 cloves garlic, minced
- 1/2 cup crumbled feta cheese (use vegan feta if needed)
- 1/4 cup Greek yogurt (use vegan yogurt if needed)
- 1 tbsp lemon juice
- 1 tsp lemon zest
- 1 tbsp fresh parsley, chopped
- 1 tbsp fresh mint, chopped
- Salt and pepper to taste
- Olive oil spray

Cauliflower Gnocchi with Marinara Dipping Sauce

Cauliflower gnocchi has become a popular low-carb alternative to traditional potato gnocchi. By using cauliflower and almond flour, this dish provides a nutrient-dense option that is both gluten-free and vegan-friendly. Air frying the gnocchi ensures they are crispy on the outside while remaining tender on the inside. Paired with a homemade marinara sauce, this dish combines classic Italian flavors with a healthy twist, making it a delightful appetizer or main course.

Nutrition Cal 220; Protein 8 g; Fat 10 g; Carb 25 g

Instructions

1. Steam the cauliflower florets until tender, about 10 minutes. Let them cool slightly.
2. Place the steamed cauliflower in a food processor and blend until smooth. Transfer to a clean kitchen towel and squeeze out as much moisture as possible.
3. In a large bowl, combine the cauliflower puree, almond flour, tapioca flour, nutritional yeast, garlic powder, salt, pepper, and egg. Mix until a dough forms.
4. On a floured surface, divide the dough into smaller portions and roll each portion into a long rope about 1/2 inch in diameter.
5. Cut the ropes into 1-inch pieces to form the gnocchi. If desired, use a fork to press gently on each piece to create ridges.
6. Preheat your air fryer to 375°F (190°C).
7. Lightly spray the air fryer basket with olive oil spray.
8. Place the gnocchi in the air fryer basket in a single layer. Lightly spray the tops with olive oil spray.
9. Cook for 12-15 minutes, shaking the basket halfway through, until the gnocchi are golden brown and crispy.
10. While the gnocchi are cooking, heat olive oil in a saucepan over medium heat.
11. Add the minced garlic and finely chopped onion, and sauté until fragrant and softened, about 3-4 minutes.
12. Add the crushed tomatoes, dried oregano, dried basil, salt, and pepper. Simmer for 10 minutes, stirring occasionally.
13. Adjust seasoning to taste.
14. Transfer the cooked gnocchi to a serving platter.
15. Garnish the marinara sauce with fresh basil and serve as a dipping sauce alongside the gnocchi.

 Prep time: 20 min

 Cook time: 15 min

 Servings: 4

Ingredients

- 1 medium head of cauliflower, cut into florets
- 1 cup almond flour (or gluten-free flour)
- 1/4 cup tapioca flour
- 1/4 cup nutritional yeast
- 1 tsp garlic powder
- 1/2 tsp salt
- 1/4 tsp black pepper
- 1 large egg (or flax egg for vegan)
- Olive oil spray

For the Marinara Dipping Sauce:
- 1 can (14.5 oz) crushed tomatoes
- 2 cloves garlic, minced
- 1/4 cup onion, finely chopped
- 1 tbsp olive oil
- 1 tsp dried oregano
- 1 tsp dried basil
- Salt and pepper to taste
- 1 tbsp fresh basil, chopped (for garnish)

DESSERTS

Fig and Walnut Halva

Halva is a traditional dessert found in many cultures across the Mediterranean, Middle East, and South Asia. It is typically made from sesame paste (tahini) and sweeteners, and can be flavored with various nuts, spices, and fruits. This air-fried version combines the natural sweetness of figs with the nutty flavors of walnuts and almond flour, creating a delightful and nutritious treat. Air frying the halva balls adds a slight crispiness, enhancing the texture and making them a unique and delicious dessert option.

Nutrition Cal 220; Protein 4 g; Fat 14 g; Carb 22 g

Instructions

1. In a food processor, combine the chopped figs, walnuts, almond flour, tahini, honey (or maple syrup), vanilla extract, ground cinnamon, ground cardamom, and a pinch of salt.
2. Process until the mixture forms a sticky, cohesive dough.
3. Using your hands, roll the mixture into small balls, about 1 inch in diameter. Place the balls on a plate or baking sheet.
4. Preheat your air fryer to 350°F (175°C).
5. Lightly spray the air fryer basket with olive oil spray.
6. Place the halva balls in the air fryer basket in a single layer, making sure they do not touch.
7. Lightly spray the tops of the halva balls with olive oil spray.
8. Cook for 8-10 minutes, shaking the basket halfway through, until the halva balls are golden brown and slightly crispy on the outside.
9. Once cooked, remove the halva balls from the air fryer and let them cool slightly.
10. Serve warm or at room temperature.

 Prep time: 15 min

 Cook time: 10 min

 Servings: 4

Ingredients

- o 1 cup dried figs, stems removed and chopped
- o 1/2 cup walnuts, chopped
- o 1/2 cup almond flour
- o 1/4 cup tahini
- o 2 tbsp honey (or maple syrup for vegan)
- o 1 tsp vanilla extract
- o 1/2 tsp ground cinnamon
- o 1/4 tsp ground cardamom
- o Pinch of salt
- o Olive oil spray

Almond and Orange Biscotti

Biscotti, which means "twice-baked" in Italian, are a classic Italian cookie known for their crunchy texture. Traditionally, biscotti are baked twice to achieve their signature crispness. This air-fried version of almond and orange biscotti retains the traditional flavor and texture but uses less energy and time. The combination of almonds and orange zest gives these biscotti a delightful Mediterranean flavor, perfect for dipping into coffee or tea. Enjoy these delicious and aromatic biscotti as a treat or a light dessert.

Nutrition   Cal 150; Protein 4 g; Fat 9 g; Carb 16 g

Instructions

1. In a large bowl, combine the almond flour, all-purpose flour, granulated sugar, baking powder, and salt. Mix well.
2. In another bowl, whisk together the eggs, olive oil, vanilla extract, and orange zest until well combined.
3. Add the wet ingredients to the dry ingredients and mix until a dough forms.
4. Fold in the sliced almonds.
5. On a lightly floured surface, divide the dough in half.
6. Shape each half into a log about 10 inches long and 2 inches wide.
7. Flatten the logs slightly.
8. Preheat your air fryer to 320°F (160°C).
9. Lightly spray the air fryer basket with olive oil spray.
10. Place one of the logs in the air fryer basket. (You may need to do this in batches depending on the size of your air fryer.)
11. Cook for 10-12 minutes, until the log is firm to the touch and lightly golden.
12. Remove the log from the air fryer and let it cool for 10 minutes.
13. Repeat with the second log.
14. Once the logs have cooled, use a sharp knife to slice them diagonally into 1/2-inch thick biscotti slices.
15. Place the slices back in the air fryer basket in a single layer.
16. Cook for an additional 8-10 minutes, flipping halfway through, until the biscotti are golden brown and crisp.
17. Remove the biscotti from the air fryer and let them cool completely on a wire rack.

 Prep time: 20 min

 Cook time: 20 min

 Servings:12

Ingredients

- o 1 1/4 cups almond flour
- o 1 cup all-purpose flour (or gluten-free flour)
- o 1/2 cup granulated sugar
- o 1 tsp baking powder
- o 1/4 tsp salt
- o 2 large eggs
- o 1/4 cup olive oil
- o 1 tsp vanilla extract
- o 1 tbsp orange zest
- o 1/2 cup sliced almonds
- o Olive oil spray

Greek Honey and Nut Phyllo Rolls

Phyllo dough, also known as filo, is a staple in Mediterranean and Middle Eastern cuisine. Its paper-thin layers become incredibly crispy when baked or air-fried. This recipe for Greek honey and nut phyllo rolls is inspired by the traditional dessert baklava, which features layers of phyllo dough, nuts, and honey syrup. By air frying the rolls, you achieve a similar crispiness with less oil and in less time. The combination of mixed nuts and warm spices, sweetened with honey syrup, makes these phyllo rolls a delicious and elegant dessert.

Nutrition   Cal 200; Protein 3 g; Fat 12 g; Carb 22 g

Instructions

1. In a medium bowl, combine the finely chopped nuts, honey, ground cinnamon, ground nutmeg, and ground cloves. Mix well.
2. Preheat your air fryer to 350°F (175°C).
3. On a clean, dry surface, lay out one sheet of phyllo dough and brush it lightly with melted butter. Place another sheet on top and brush it with butter as well.
4. Repeat until you have layered four sheets of phyllo dough, brushing each layer with butter.
5. Cut the layered phyllo dough into four equal strips.
6. Place a tablespoon of the nut mixture at the end of each strip.
7. Roll up the phyllo dough, starting from the end with the filling, and tuck in the sides as you roll to form a neat roll.
8. Lightly spray the air fryer basket with olive oil spray.
9. Place the phyllo rolls in the air fryer basket, seam side down, in a single layer. Lightly spray the tops with olive oil.
10. Air fry the phyllo rolls for 12-15 minutes, turning halfway through, until they are golden brown and crispy.
11. While the rolls are cooking, combine the honey, water, lemon juice, lemon zest, and cinnamon stick in a small saucepan.
12. Bring to a boil over medium heat, then reduce the heat and simmer for 5 minutes. Remove from heat and let it cool slightly.
13. Once the phyllo rolls are cooked, remove them from the air fryer and place them on a serving platter.
14. Drizzle the warm honey syrup over the rolls.
15. Serve warm or at room temperature.

 Prep time: 20 min

 Cook time: 20 min

 Servings:12

Ingredients

- 1 cup mixed nuts (such as walnuts, almonds, and pistachios), finely chopped
- 1/4 cup honey
- 1 tsp ground cinnamon
- 1/2 tsp ground nutmeg
- 1/4 tsp ground cloves
- 1 package phyllo dough, thawed
- 1/2 cup melted butter (use vegan butter if needed)
- Olive oil spray

For the Honey Syrup:
- 1/2 cup honey
- 1/4 cup water
- 1 tbsp lemon juice
- 1 tsp lemon zest
- 1 cinnamon stick

Fig and Pistachio Frangipane Tart

Frangipane is a sweet almond-flavored filling made from almonds, butter, sugar, and eggs, often used in tarts and pastries. This recipe puts a Mediterranean twist on the classic frangipane tart by incorporating pistachios and figs. Pistachios add a rich, nutty flavor, while figs provide natural sweetness and a unique texture. Air frying the tart gives it a beautifully crisp crust and evenly cooked filling, making it a perfect dessert for any occasion.

Nutrition
Cal 350; Protein 6 g; Fat 22 g; Carb 32 g

Instructions

1. In a food processor, combine the all-purpose flour and powdered sugar. Add the cold butter and pulse until the mixture resembles coarse crumbs.
2. Add the egg yolk and pulse a few times. Gradually add cold water, one tablespoon at a time, and pulse until the dough comes together.
3. Shape the dough into a disk, wrap it in plastic wrap, and refrigerate for at least 30 minutes.
4. Preheat your air fryer to 350°F (175°C).
5. In a bowl, cream together the softened butter and sugar until light and fluffy.
6. Add the ground pistachios, almond flour, egg, vanilla extract, and almond extract. Mix until well combined.
7. Roll out the tart crust on a lightly floured surface to fit your tart pan.
8. Place the crust in the tart pan, pressing it into the bottom and sides. Trim any excess dough.
9. Spread the pistachio frangipane evenly over the tart crust.
10. Arrange the sliced figs on top of the frangipane in a decorative pattern.
11. Place the tart pan in the air fryer basket.
12. Air fry for 15-20 minutes, or until the crust is golden and the frangipane is set.
13. Once cooked, remove the tart from the air fryer and let it cool slightly.
14. Drizzle the tart with honey and sprinkle with chopped pistachios.
15. Serve warm or at room temperature.

 Prep time: 30 min

 Cook time: 15 min

 Servings:8

Ingredients

For the Tart Crust:
- 1 1/4 cups all-purpose flour (use gluten-free flour if needed)
- 1/4 cup powdered sugar
- 1/2 cup cold butter, cubed (use vegan butter if needed)
- 1 egg yolk (or flax egg for vegan)
- 1-2 tbsp cold water

For the Pistachio Frangipane:
- 1/2 cup unsalted pistachios, finely ground
- 1/4 cup almond flour
- 1/4 cup sugar
- 1/4 cup butter, softened (use vegan butter if needed)
- 1 egg (or flax egg for vegan)
- 1 tsp vanilla extract
- 1/4 tsp almond extract

For the Topping:
- 6-8 fresh figs, sliced
- 1/4 cup chopped pistachios
- 2 tbsp honey (or maple syrup for vegan)

Rose Water and Pistachio Semolina Cake

Semolina is a coarse flour made from durum wheat, commonly used in Mediterranean and Middle Eastern desserts. It gives cakes a unique, slightly grainy texture and a rich flavor. Rose water, made from distilling rose petals, adds a delicate floral aroma and taste to the cake, making it a luxurious and fragrant dessert. This rose water and pistachio semolina cake is a beautiful blend of flavors and textures, perfect for special occasions or as an exotic treat.

Nutrition   Cal 350; Protein 6 g; Fat 18 g; Carb 42 g

Instructions

1. In a large bowl, combine the semolina flour, all-purpose flour, sugar, baking powder, baking soda, and salt. Mix well.
2. Add the melted butter, yogurt, rose water, and finely chopped pistachios to the dry ingredients. Mix until well combined and a thick batter forms.
3. Preheat your air fryer to 320°F (160°C).
4. 3.Prepare the Cake Pan:
5. Grease an air fryer-safe cake pan with butter or oil.
6. Pour the batter into the prepared cake pan and smooth the top with a spatula.
7. Place the cake pan in the air fryer basket.
8. Air fry for 25-30 minutes, or until a toothpick inserted into the center comes out clean and the top is golden brown.
9. If the top browns too quickly, cover it with aluminum foil and continue cooking until done.
10. While the cake is baking, combine the sugar, water, and lemon juice in a small saucepan.
11. Bring to a boil over medium heat, stirring until the sugar is dissolved.
12. Remove from heat and stir in the rose water. Set aside to cool slightly.
13. Once the cake is cooked, remove it from the air fryer and let it cool for 10 minutes.
14. Pour the warm syrup over the cake, allowing it to soak in. Let the cake cool completely in the pan.
15. Once the cake is completely cooled and the syrup is absorbed, remove it from the pan.
16. Garnish with finely chopped pistachios and dried rose petals if desired.
17. Slice and serve.

 Prep time: 20 min

 Cook time: 30 min

 Servings:8

Ingredients

For the Cake:
- o 1 cup semolina flour
- o 1/2 cup all-purpose flour (use gluten-free flour if needed)
- o 1 cup sugar
- o 1/2 cup unsalted butter, melted (use vegan butter if needed)
- o 1 cup plain yogurt (use vegan yogurt if needed)
- o 1/2 cup finely chopped pistachios
- o 2 tbsp rose water
- o 1 tsp baking powder
- o 1/2 tsp baking soda
- o Pinch of salt

For the Syrup:
- o 1/2 cup sugar
- o 1/2 cup water
- o 1 tbsp rose water
- o 1 tbsp lemon juice

For Garnish:
- o 2 tbsp finely chopped pistachios

Ricotta and Lemon Zest Fritters

Ricotta cheese, known for its creamy texture and mild flavor, is a versatile ingredient often used in both savory and sweet dishes. The addition of lemon zest to these fritters provides a refreshing citrus aroma that complements the richness of the ricotta. Air frying the fritters results in a light and fluffy texture with a slightly crispy exterior, making them a delightful treat for breakfast or dessert. This method also uses less oil than traditional frying, making the fritters a healthier option. Enjoy these delicious ricotta and lemon zest fritters with your favorite toppings for a special treat.

Nutrition   Cal 250; Protein 10 g; Fat 10 g; Carb 30 g

Instructions

1. In a large bowl, combine the ricotta cheese, lightly beaten eggs, sugar, vanilla extract, and lemon zest. Mix well until smooth.
2. In another bowl, whisk together the flour, baking powder, and salt.
3. Gradually add the dry ingredients to the wet mixture, stirring until just combined. The batter should be thick but smooth.
4. Preheat your air fryer to 350°F (175°C).
5. Using a tablespoon or small cookie scoop, drop spoonfuls of batter onto a parchment-lined tray. Shape into small balls if necessary.
6. Lightly spray the air fryer basket with olive oil spray.
7. Place the fritters in the air fryer basket in a single layer, making sure they do not touch.
8. Lightly spray the tops of the fritters with olive oil.
9. Air fry for 8-10 minutes, turning halfway through, until the fritters are golden brown and cooked through.
10. Once cooked, remove the fritters from the air fryer and let them cool slightly.
11. Dust with powdered sugar if desired.
12. Serve warm with honey or maple syrup and fresh berries on the side.

 Prep time: 15 min

 Cook time: 10 min

 Servings:4

Ingredients

- 1 cup ricotta cheese
- 2 eggs, lightly beaten
- 1/4 cup sugar
- 1 tsp vanilla extract
- 1 tbsp lemon zest
- 1 cup all-purpose flour (use gluten-free flour if needed)
- 1 tsp baking powder
- Pinch of salt
- Olive oil spray
- Powdered sugar for dusting (optional)

For Serving:

- Honey or maple syrup
Fresh berries (optional)

Bananas and Stuffed Figs

Bananas and figs are both rich in dietary fiber, vitamins, and minerals, making them nutritious as well as delicious. Air frying these fruits enhances their natural sweetness and creates a delightful caramelized exterior. The combination of creamy cheese and crunchy nuts in the stuffed figs adds a wonderful contrast in textures, while the honey or maple syrup provides a touch of sweetness. This dessert is a perfect example of how simple ingredients can be transformed into a gourmet treat using an air fryer, making it an ideal dish for entertaining or enjoying as a healthy indulgence.

Nutrition   Cal 250; Protein 4 g; Fat 10 g; Carb 38 g

Instructions

1. In a small bowl, mix the honey or maple syrup with the ground cinnamon.
2. Lightly brush the banana slices with the honey-cinnamon mixture.
3. Using a small spoon, fill each fig half with about 1/2 teaspoon of goat cheese or vegan cream cheese.
4. Top each stuffed fig with chopped walnuts or pecans.
5. Drizzle with honey or maple syrup and sprinkle with ground cinnamon.
6. Preheat your air fryer to 350°F (175°C).
7. Lightly spray the air fryer basket with olive oil spray.
8. Place the banana slices in the air fryer basket in a single layer.
9. Air fry for 5-7 minutes, until the bananas are golden brown and caramelized. Remove and set aside.
10. Place the stuffed figs in the air fryer basket in a single layer.
11. Air fry for 5-7 minutes, until the figs are tender and the cheese is slightly melted.
12. Arrange the air-fried bananas and stuffed figs on a serving platter.
13. Drizzle with additional honey or maple syrup if desired.
14. Serve warm.

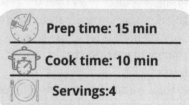

Prep time: 15 min

Cook time: 10 min

Servings:4

Ingredients

- 2 ripe bananas, sliced lengthwise and then halved
- 2 tbsp honey or maple syrup
- 1/2 tsp ground cinnamon
- Olive oil spray

For the Stuffed Figs:

- 8 fresh figs, stems removed and halved
- 1/4 cup goat cheese or vegan cream cheese
- 1/4 cup chopped walnuts or pecans
- 1 tbsp honey or maple syrup
- 1/2 tsp ground cinnamon

Apple Chips

Apple chips are a healthy and delicious snack that can be enjoyed any time of the day. Air frying the apple slices requires much less oil compared to traditional frying methods, resulting in a low-calorie snack that retains the natural sweetness and nutrients of the apples. The combination of cinnamon and apples is not only tasty but also provides a warm, comforting aroma that makes these chips irresistible. Perfect for lunchboxes, snacks, or a crunchy topping for yogurt and oatmeal, air-fried apple chips are a versatile treat that everyone will love.

Nutrition   Cal 60; Protein 0 g; Fat 0 g; Carb 16 g

Instructions

1. Wash and core the apples. Using a mandoline slicer or a sharp knife, slice the apples into thin rounds, about 1/8-inch thick.
2. If desired, mix the ground cinnamon and sugar (if using) in a small bowl.
3. Preheat your air fryer to 300°F (150°C).
4. Lightly spray the apple slices with olive oil spray.
5. Sprinkle both sides of the apple slices with the cinnamon mixture, making sure they are evenly coated.
6. Place the apple slices in the air fryer basket in a single layer. You may need to do this in batches depending on the size of your air fryer.
7. Air fry for 15-20 minutes, flipping the slices halfway through, until the apple chips are crisp and golden brown. Keep an eye on them towards the end of the cooking time to prevent burning.
8. Remove the apple chips from the air fryer and let them cool on a wire rack. They will continue to crisp up as they cool.
9. Serve immediately or store in an airtight container for up to a week.

 Prep time: 10 min

 Cook time: 15 min

 Servings:4

Ingredients

- 2 large apples (any variety)
- 1 tsp ground cinnamon
- 1 tsp sugar or sweetener of choice (optional)
- Olive oil spray

Lemon and Olive Oil Cake

Lemon and olive oil cake is a classic Mediterranean dessert known for its moist texture and bright, tangy flavor. Olive oil adds a rich, fruity note to the cake while keeping it tender and moist. The combination of lemon juice and zest provides a refreshing citrus aroma that complements the olive oil perfectly. Air frying the cake allows it to cook evenly and develop a lovely golden crust, making it a delightful treat for any occasion. This cake is perfect for those who appreciate simple yet elegant desserts with a touch of Mediterranean flair.

Nutrition   Cal 300; Protein 4 g; Fat 14 g; Carb 42 g

Instructions

1. In a large bowl, whisk together the flour, granulated sugar, baking powder, baking soda, and salt.
2. In another bowl, combine the olive oil, Greek yogurt, eggs, lemon juice, lemon zest, and vanilla extract. Mix well until smooth.
3. Gradually add the wet ingredients to the dry ingredients, stirring until just combined. Be careful not to overmix.
4. Preheat your air fryer to 320°F (160°C).
5. Grease an air fryer-safe cake pan with olive oil or non-stick spray.
6. Pour the batter into the prepared cake pan and smooth the top with a spatula.
7. Place the cake pan in the air fryer basket.
8. Air fry for 25-30 minutes, or until a toothpick inserted into the center comes out clean and the top is golden brown.
9. If the top browns too quickly, cover it with aluminum foil and continue cooking until done.
10. While the cake is baking, whisk together the powdered sugar and lemon juice in a small bowl until smooth and thick. Adjust the consistency with more lemon juice if necessary.
11. Once the cake is cooked, remove it from the air fryer and let it cool in the pan for 10 minutes.
12. Remove the cake from the pan and place it on a wire rack to cool completely.
13. Drizzle the lemon glaze over the cooled cake, allowing it to drip down the sides.
14. Slice and serve the lemon and olive oil cake.
15. Enjoy with a cup of tea or coffee.

 Prep time: 15 min

 Cook time: 30 min

 Servings:8

Ingredients

- 1 1/2 cups all-purpose flour (use gluten-free flour if needed)
- 1 cup granulated sugar
- 1/2 tsp baking powder
- 1/2 tsp baking soda
- 1/4 tsp salt
- 1/2 cup extra virgin olive oil
- 1/2 cup plain Greek yogurt (use vegan yogurt if needed)
- 3 large eggs (or flax eggs for vegan)
- 1/4 cup fresh lemon juice
- 1 tbsp lemon zest
- 1 tsp vanilla extract

For the Glaze:
- 1 cup powdered sugar
- 2-3 tbsp fresh lemon juice

Almond Banana with Honey and Nuts

Bananas are rich in potassium, fiber, and essential vitamins, making them a nutritious and energizing snack. Combining them with almond butter adds healthy fats and protein, while the nuts provide a satisfying crunch and additional nutrients. Honey, a natural sweetener with antioxidant properties, enhances the flavors and brings everything together. This air-fried almond banana dish is a delicious and wholesome treat that can be enjoyed as a dessert, snack, or even a quick breakfast. The warm bananas paired with the crunchy nuts and sweet honey create a delightful and comforting combination.

Nutrition   Cal 200; Protein 3 g; Fat 8 g; Carb 32 g

Instructions

1. Preheat your air fryer to 350°F (175°C).
2. Arrange the banana halves on a plate or tray.
3. Spread a thin layer of almond butter on each banana half.
4. Drizzle the honey evenly over the almond butter-covered bananas.
5. Sprinkle the chopped mixed nuts and ground cinnamon on top.
6. Lightly spray the air fryer basket with olive oil spray.
7. Carefully place the prepared banana halves in the air fryer basket in a single layer.
8. Air fry for 8-10 minutes, or until the bananas are warm and the nuts are lightly toasted. Keep an eye on them to prevent burning.
9. Remove the bananas from the air fryer and let them cool slightly.
10. Serve warm, drizzled with a little extra honey if desired.

 Prep time: 10 min

 Cook time: 10 min

 Servings:4

Ingredients

- 4 ripe bananas, peeled and halved lengthwise
- 2 tbsp almond butter
- 2 tbsp honey (or maple syrup for vegan)
- 1/4 cup chopped mixed nuts (such as almonds, walnuts, and pecans)
- 1/2 tsp ground cinnamon
- Olive oil spray

Conclusion

Embarking on a journey to a healthier lifestyle can be both exciting and fulfilling, especially when it involves delicious, wholesome food. The Mediterranean diet, with its rich flavors and proven health benefits, offers a simple yet effective way to nourish your body and soul. By incorporating the versatility and convenience of an air fryer, you can enjoy all the advantages of this time-honored way of eating with the added benefit of quicker cooking times and easier cleanup.

Throughout this book, you've discovered how the Mediterranean diet's focus on fresh vegetables, whole grains, lean proteins, and healthy fats can transform your meals and your health. You've learned how to maximize the potential of your air fryer to create dishes that are not only good for you but also bursting with flavor. From crispy appetizers to satisfying main dishes and even delightful desserts, the air fryer proves to be a perfect companion in your Mediterranean kitchen.

As you continue to explore and enjoy these recipes, remember that the Mediterranean diet is more than just a way of eating—it's a lifestyle. It encourages you to savor your food, share meals with loved ones, and stay active. By embracing this approach, you're not just making a temporary change but adopting a sustainable, enjoyable way of living that supports long-term health and happiness.

May this book inspire you to keep experimenting in the kitchen, trying new recipes, and making the most of your air fryer. Here's to delicious, healthy meals that nourish your body and bring joy to your table every day. Enjoy the journey!

2024

Anthony Green

Made in the USA
Coppell, TX
26 October 2024

39204724R00072